LONG PLAYERS

LONG PLAYERS

Writers on the Albums That
Shaped Them

EDITED BY
TOM GATTI

BLOOMSBURY PUBLISHING
LONDON · OXFORD · NEW YORK · NEW DELHI · SYDNEY

BLOOMSBURY PUBLISHING
Bloomsbury Publishing Plc
50 Bedford Square, London, WC1B 3DP, UK
29 Earlsfort Terrace, Dublin 2, Ireland

BLOOMSBURY, BLOOMSBURY PUBLISHING and the Diana logo are
trademarks of Bloomsbury Publishing Plc

First published in Great Britain 2021
Introduction copyright © Tom Gatti, 2021
Individual chapters copyright © the Contributors, 2021
(further details can be found on pp. 207–9)

Tom Gatti and the Contributors have asserted their right under the Copyright,
Designs and Patents Act, 1988, to be identified as Author of this work

For legal purposes the Acknowledgements on p. 213
constitute an extension of this copyright page

Quotation from 'A Natural Disaster' by Anathema reproduced with
permission. Lyrics written by D. Cavanagh, published by Concord Music.

Quotation from 'Roundabout' by Yes used by permission of Hal Leonard
Europe Limited. Words & Music by Steve Howe & Jon Anderson, © Copyright
1980 Universal Music Publishing Limited. All Rights Reserved. International
Copyright Secured.

A catalogue record for this book is available from the British Library

ISBN: HB: 978-1-5266-2578-6; EBOOK: 978-1-5266-2577-9

2 4 6 8 10 9 7 5 3 1

Typeset by Newgen KnowledgeWorks Pvt. Ltd., Chennai, India
Printed and bound in Great Britain by CPI Group (UK) Ltd, Croydon CRO 4YY

To find out more about our authors and books visit www.bloomsbury.com
and sign up for our newsletters

CONTENTS

Introduction

When I discovered the album, it was a form already past its prime. Michael Jackson's *Thriller* was released in November 1982, a few months after my first birthday. By the end of 1983, it had sold 22 million copies worldwide. Until then, no album by a solo artist had sold more than 12 million.[1] Almost forty years later, its sales total – more than 50 million – is still unbeaten. But, fittingly for a record concerned with corpses and tombs, *Thriller* sounded the death-knell for the reign of the long player. The rock writer David Hepworth has suggested that it marked the point at which making records 'changed from an art to a science.'[2] Issued at the end of the vinyl era, it was the last album to truly conquer the world.

Not that I knew any of that when, aged seven, I pulled the record from the shelf and lay on my stomach on the carpet of our suburban sitting room. The poise of the 24-year-old Jackson, reclining in his white suit with its faintly otherworldly glow, was impressive enough. But flipping open the gatefold revealed a tiger cub on Jackson's knee – a delightful surprise, and considering that my favourite piece of vinyl up to this point had been the soundtrack of *The Jungle Book*, subconsciously reassuring. Pulling out the inner sleeve, I was met with a dense grid of lyrics. As the hyperactive drum track and propulsive bass of 'Wanna Be Startin' Somethin'' kicked in, I read along, appreciative of Jackson's habit of thorough and accurate transcription (every 'yeah, yeah' is present and correct), perplexed by the language (who is 'a vegetable' and why?) and intrigued by the weird line drawings. (One depicted Michael and another chap – Paul McCartney, I later discovered – each wearing matching tank tops and pulling the arm of an Olive Oyl-like figure, as if about to tear her in two; the other showed Michael and his paramour on a sofa, encircled by a pair of werewolf arms extending from the television screen.)

I didn't know that this was an 'album' but it seemed to me an object full of rich meanings, a text to be deciphered, and a sound-world in which to lose myself. A year or so and many listens later, I went to a disco at my primary school and brought *Thriller* to lend to the DJ (misunderstanding the process, or simply not having much faith in his record collection). He humoured me, obligingly giving 'Billie Jean' a spin – and when he returned the album, he generously slipped something in the sleeve: his own 7-inch of 'Smooth Criminal'. On the reverse of the sleeve was an inset image of Michael in a black leather jacket adorned with buckles and zips, and the fateful words: 'Also available: Michael Jackson's LP *Bad*'. The golden age of the LP might have been over, but for me it had just begun.

*

The gramophone record, made of heavy, brittle shellac and spinning at 78 revolutions per minute (rpm), dominated recorded music for fifty years. Emile Berliner, a German who had left the Franco-Prussian War behind to move to the US,[3] secured a patent in 1887 for a gramophone[4] – the first player to use flat discs with a spiral groove. Initially the playing time was two crackly minutes per side. As technology developed, this eventually increased to four minutes, but even then, listening to a full piece of classical music meant loading a succession of records. These discs, manufacturers realised, could be stored in something resembling a book of stamps or photographs: the German Odeon label introduced the term 'album' in 1909, when it released *The Nutcracker Suite* in a wallet containing four records.[5]

Through the thirties and forties, the holy grail for the record companies was a format with extended listening time: a 'long player'. A 33⅓ rpm vinyl disc was produced as early as 1932, but it took another sixteen years for the materials to be perfected and, crucially, a length to be settled on. After the Second World War, when the technology was in place, Edward Wallerstein, the president of Columbia Records, was offered prototype discs of between seven and twelve minutes per side. But after a week exploring the label's classical backlist, he settled on a figure of no less than seventeen minutes per side – long enough for most classical works to be contained on a single record. The final product was twelve inches in diameter and twenty-two and a half minutes a side, and when it was launched in 1948 the 'Revolutionary Disk Marvel' lived up to its name.[6]

It would be two decades before a new generation of musicians figured out how to turn this format, designed to carry *The Mikado* and *South Pacific*, into a modern work of art – a marvel for the baby boomer generation. Initially, albums were synonymous with 'grown-up' music: classical and jazz for the musos; soundtracks and comedy recordings for those in search of light entertainment. The rise of rock and roll in the fifties and beat music in the early sixties was driven by singles, disseminated through the radio and jukeboxes and bought with pocket money or Saturday-job cash on 45 rpm 7-inch records. Albums were a by-product, a commercial afterthought stuffed with filler and sold only to fans who were sufficiently devoted or wealthy: Phil Spector, the producer most responsible for shaping the sound of the early sixties, memorably described LPs as 'two hits and ten pieces of junk'.[7]

4

But by 1965, this had begun to change. In that year the Beatles released their sixth album, *Rubber Soul* – a mature, experimental and ambitious record, containing no cover versions and very little filler (unfortunately Ringo's country number 'What Goes On' prevents it being certified padding-free). The band's American record label Capitol did not release any singles in advance, giving the album the air of an unusually coherent artistic work. Listeners agreed. John Cale and Lou Reed were galvanised by *Rubber Soul* in their newly christened group the Velvet Underground;[8] the Rolling Stones ditched their R&B covers and recorded *Aftermath*; and Brian Wilson of the Beach Boys rushed to begin work on his own 'complete statement',[9] *Pet Sounds*.

Considering Spector's views on the album form, it's ironic that Wilson's LP, released in May 1966, was partly an attempt to sustain his version of Spector's 'Wall of Sound' approach over a whole record. 'It wasn't really a *song* concept album, or *lyrically* a concept album,' Wilson later said; 'it was really a *production* concept album.'[10] *Pet Sounds*' song cycle married emotionally naked lyrics with a rich symphonic sound; at times it is almost unbearably beautiful. Paul McCartney declared it 'the album of all time' and acknowledged that the Beatles needed to raise their game yet again.[11] The result was *Sgt. Pepper's Lonely Hearts Club Band*.

If *Pet Sounds* and rock's first double albums – Bob Dylan's *Blonde on Blonde* and *Freak Out!* by the Mothers of Invention – had pushed the LP further away from a ragbag of songs and towards a unified whole, the Beatles' eighth album, released in June 1967, completed the transformation. The alter-ego of the 'fake group' allowed them to 'make up all the culture around it and collect all our heroes in one place'.[12] There was the autobiographical through-line of a Liverpudlian childhood; the sonic portrayal of psychedelic drugs; the audacious segues from track to track; Peter Blake's myth-making cover art: *Sgt. Pepper* was not simply a very good album – it was, wrote Kenneth Tynan in *The Times*, a 'decisive moment in the history of Western civilisation'.[13] It was twenty years ago today, McCartney told us, that Sgt. Pepper taught the band to play; it had also been twenty years since the long player was born. The technology developed to contain a Beethoven symphony had spawned an entirely new form.

In 1969, just two years after *Sgt. Pepper*'s release, albums outsold singles for the first time in Britain. The tables had turned: the 7-inch discs that had powered pop music's rise were now seen as commercial and disposable. As Bob Stanley points out in *Yeah Yeah Yeah: The Story of Modern Pop*,[14] the British number ones of 1970 show the split between the two formats. Apart from Simon & Garfunkel, none of the artists who achieved number one albums – Pink Floyd, Led Zeppelin, Bob Dylan – trouble the singles list, which is full of unhip fare such as Edison Lighthouse's 'Love Grows (Where My Rosemary Goes)' and Dana's Eurovision-winner 'All Kinds of Everything'.

The following year, album releases included Carole King's *Tapestry*, Marvin Gaye's *What's Going On* and Joni Mitchell's *Blue*.

*

By the age of fourteen, I'd been through several Walkmans. My cassette of *Bad*, promptly obtained after that disco, had worn thin and been temporarily retired: I'd given as much attention to its detailed multi-fold inlay ('Michael Jackson's heartbeat recording by Dr Eric Chevlen') as I had done to the sleeve of *Thriller*. Meanwhile, I'd moved through the entire Beatles back catalogue, via my dad's vinyl, and then on to the heavier sounds of Guns N' Roses, Nirvana and Cypress Hill. In 1994 my bedroom was furnished with a boom-box CD player, and the first three discs in my collection were Green Day's *Dookie*, Warren G's *Regulate ... G Funk Era* (won in a competition in the *Guardian*) and Elastica's self-titled debut; around the same time I bought Tricky's *Maxinquaye* on cassette. Cartoon punk, West Coast rap, angular Britpop and paranoid trip-hop: I had limited funds but unlimited curiosity, and was keen to explore my options. Then came *The Bends*.

In the first few seconds of Radiohead's second album there's a sound like a wind whistling through a nuclear winter; metaphorically at least, it keeps blowing until the end of 'Street Spirit (Fade Out)' at the record's close. Though its more sophisticated successor, *OK Computer*, has a stronger claim to being a concept album, *The Bends* portrayed a dystopia that was recognisably close to the present. You could see it in the grainy quality of the resuscitation mannequin on the cover, described by the artist Stanley Donwood, who took the photograph, as having 'a facial expression like that of an android discovering for the first time the sensations of ecstasy and agony, simultaneously'.[15] You could sense it from the song titles: 'Fake Plastic Trees', 'My Iron Lung', 'Black Star'. Once you started listening, you could find it in Thom Yorke's bruised and resigned vocals, the background layers of shimmering and stuttering guitar-work and the lyrics that married doomed relationships with the ennui of late twentieth-century capitalism. This was an album to immerse yourself in; to me as a teenager, it was as much of a 'complete statement' as *Pet Sounds* or *Sgt. Pepper*. What's more, it acknowledges, in its title track, the idea of a vanished golden age: the song's narrator wishes it was the sixties. He probably wishes too that he wasn't on a digital format, housed in a plastic case, released by a major corporate label, on a rapidly degrading planet. But if not, what would he have to sing about?

*

The compact disc gets a bad press. David Hepworth describes buying a CD in a megastore in the nineties as 'more akin to an act of surrender than to an expression of devotion'.[16] When the novelist Bret Easton Ellis imagined

8

a yuppie serial killer, he made him a CD collector: in *American Psycho*, Patrick Bateman is an obsessive fan of Phil Collins and Huey Lewis and the News and takes great care of his compact discs (he has several players and a laser lens cleaner). Most people agree on the CD's flaws: its over-sanitised sound lacks the warmth of vinyl; its size doesn't allow for the glorious artwork of the seventies; its digital playback lacks ceremony; its extended running time leads to bloated works; you can't easily roll a joint on its case.

But the CD did not kill the album. On the contrary: in 1999, the music industry had staggering revenues of $27.8 billion worldwide.[17] In 2000, 942.5 million CD albums were sold in the US, compared to 344 million LPs at vinyl's peak in 1977.[18] In the age of the compact disc, we were buying more albums than ever before. At which point the Golden Ager replies: Aha! But they were on CD, so you weren't listening to them properly. And if you did listen to them properly, you'd discover that they weren't very good.

It's true that the CD – slipping around in its optimistically named 'jewel' case, with its sad crown of snapped plastic teeth – is not a format that inspires devotion. But those of us who did not grow up in the glory days of vinyl learned to be adaptable, moving seamlessly from our parents' dusty record players to tape decks, from increasingly svelte Walkmans to cheap mini CD hi-fis and jumpy Sony Discmans, and then, for the budding

DJs, back to turntables and 12-inches. (Some of us even embraced the MiniDisc.) Technology was changing, but we weren't faced with the mid-life crisis of whether or not we should replace our entire music collection – we just carried on amassing stuff in different formats. Pushed to articulate our position, we would have said: we don't really care how it comes, just let us at the music.

And it was plentiful. The hip-hop collective Wu-Tang Clan's 1993 debut, *Enter the Wu-Tang (36 Chambers)*, created its own absorbing mythos from Shaolin kung fu films and New York grit. Jeff Buckley's *Grace* (1994) introduced a songwriter whose raw, soul-baring talent matched that of his father (Tim died at twenty-eight; Jeff lasted to thirty). DJ Shadow's *Endtroducing ...* (1996) did for the sampler what Jimi Hendrix had done for the guitar. Björk's *Homogenic* (1997) was a glorious hymn to the landscape of Iceland wrapped up in abrasive electronics and lush strings. Massive Attack's *Mezzanine* (1998) ushered the listener deep into a dark, dub-rock otherworld. The Flaming Lips' *The Soft Bulletin* (1999), a symphony of love, death, science and supermen, was a score for a film that didn't exist. Crucially, all of these works used the album format that had been established half a century before. And even though the distinction between side A and side B was lost on CD, many musicians were still thinking in terms of a first and second act – not least because most of their output was also released on vinyl and cassette.

Just like the LPs of rock's heyday, these albums offered a profound listening experience and demanded repeated replaying. They were not disposable. Yes, we sometimes picked them up in megastores, where they sat alongside the decade's monster sellers such as Alanis Morissette's *Jagged Little Pill* and the *Bodyguard* soundtrack – though we also flicked through the CD racks in tiny independent shops with just as much giddy expectation as our parents had done with vinyl. But the idea that a CD represented less of a commitment than a vinyl record is nonsense. If anything, the opposite was true: at between £10 (if you got a bargain) and £16, the notoriously overpriced compact disc was more of an outlay than the equivalent record would have been in the late sixties or early seventies. Considering the fact that in August 1997 the average pint of lager was £1.84,[19] you could have drunk yourself under the table for the price of Oasis's *Be Here Now* – though both experiences would have left you equally bloated and depressed.

In the CD era, we weighed up our purchases carefully, reading reviews in *Select* and the *NME*, and untangling the headphones from HMV's awkward listening posts – a much-reduced version of the booths that graced its stores in the fifties and sixties. Even when I didn't have much to spend, I spent it on music. Towards the end of my first year at university, my bank balance tallied £25, with two weeks left to go until term was over. But I somehow ended up in the record shop and could not bring myself to leave without two debut albums I'd read about: *Asleep in the Back* and *The Moldy Peaches*. The band behind the former, Elbow, have gone on to stadia-filling success; the Moldy Peaches haven't – but I stand by my decision that both were sound investments (and a fortnight of eating penne pasta was not too different from my usual diet anyway).

Once we'd committed to a record, we gave it more than a fair hearing. I took the English indie band Kula Shaker's second album, *Peasants, Pigs & Astronauts*, away on holiday before my A levels, attempting to convince myself that tracks such as 'Mystical Machine Gun' and 'Golden Avatar' offered a great psychedelic experience (they didn't). Perhaps this is partly why some of the era's most disappointing records (see *Be Here Now* or even Blur's *The Great Escape*) got rapturous receptions at the time: we'd all spent so much time and money on the damned things that we struggled to admit when they weren't much good.

While the album had lost none of its cachet, listening habits were changing. Though there must have been plenty of fans soaking up music alone in their bedrooms in the sixties and seventies, tales of the album's heyday tend to revolve around communal experiences. There's a gold-standard anecdote that, for me, encapsulates the notion of the LP as an inherently social medium. When the Beatles finished recording *Sgt. Pepper*, they took an early pressing to 'Mama' Cass Elliot's flat off the King's

Road. At six in the morning, they perched speakers on the window ledge and blasted the album across Chelsea. 'All the windows around us opened and people leaned out,' recalled the band's publicist, Derek Taylor. 'A lovely spring morning. People were smiling and giving us the thumbs up.'[20] In writing about this period, the pop album form becomes inseparable from the idea of a golden age: the late Ian MacDonald, who repeats Derek Taylor's story in his seminal book about the Beatles, *Revolution in the Head*, writes that 'anyone unlucky enough not to have been aged between fourteen and thirty during 1966–7 will never know the excitement of those years in popular culture. A sunny optimism permeated everything and possibilities seemed limitless.'[21]

A vinyl LP served another social function, as a highly visible calling card: a copy of *Led Zeppelin II* under your arm left nobody in any doubt of your credentials. Smaller formats put an end to this: to advertise your taste, you'd need to buy a T-shirt. Moreover, the increasing portability of music, from the advent of the Walkman in 1979 onwards, meant that you could enjoy a private listening experience in a public space. Headphones, though, did not take away from the sanctity of the album; if anything, they deepened it. Introspective, music-loving teenagers could spend their journeys to and from school on a drum'n'bass pilgrimage with Goldie's *Timeless* or drifting high above the rooftops with Spiritualized's *Ladies and Gentlemen We Are Floating in Space*, rather than endure a stream of *Fast Show* catchphrases and 'your mum' jokes from the lads and ladettes – yes, that was a thing back then too – at the back of the bus.

In the nineties, artists and fans had the enormous resource of four decades of pop music to draw on. Cool Britannia had resurrected the Beatles, whose *Anthology* series was released in 1995–6. But there were deeper seams to mine. Jason Pierce of Spiritualized stole a haunting line about a 'hole in daddy's arm' from the American country-folk singer John Prine, which left a breadcrumb trail to his 1971 debut album. Goldie's 1993 track 'Ghosts of My Life' sampled Japan's 'Ghosts' from 1981. Super Furry Animals quoted Steely Dan; Fatboy Slim nicked a riff from the Who. Jeff Buckley fans explored Tim Buckley's similarly dreamy back catalogue. Previously overlooked sixties artists such as Nick Drake and Arthur Lee of the band Love had their albums reissued on CD and were written about in magazines as if they were new discoveries – which they were, to many of us. When I first played Nick Drake's *Pink Moon*, it took my breath away: I had never heard anything quite so starkly beautiful. Over a mere twenty-eight minutes, it rendered a whole swathe of maudlin male troubadours in the so-called new acoustic movement totally irrelevant.

The album was not dying: it was in a state of constant, revivifying conversation. The artistic achievement of *Sgt. Pepper* and the cultural hegemony of *Thriller* may have remained unchallenged, but it did not feel like the end of the journey. Everywhere, there were new arterial roads opening up, new directions to explore. Unfortunately for the music industry, one of these paths led directly to the MP3.

*

The primary worry of music executives in the late nineties was the threat from bootleg CDs, the industry having failed to learn its lesson from the much-derided 'home taping is killing music' campaign of the previous decade. The technology needed to copy compact discs had become widely available: that was a genuine problem. But the more existential threat was invisible. In 1995, a century after Emile Berliner invented the gramophone record, music technology underwent a further revolution, thanks to another German engineer. Karlheinz Brandenburg had devoted thirteen years[22] to creating a digital format that could compress audio data sufficiently to make a file small enough to manage; now, finally, with the help of a working group of fellow specialists, he had the MP3. It was playable on home computers, but it had no portable device and studio engineers thought it sounded terrible. The recording industry barely looked up from its profit sheets.

But users didn't notice the decline in sound quality. And they weren't just loading their CDs to play them on their PCs, burn a copy for a friend or transfer their tracks to one of the early MP3 players (the Rio PMP300, launched in 1998, stored thirty minutes of music). They were uploading them to the internet and sharing them for free.

A small number of dedicated music pirates were doing this in a remarkably organised way, procuring CDs via a network of moles who worked in pressing plants and leaking the files online before the album's official release date. Then, in 1999, an eighteen-year-old American university dropout called Shawn Fanning launched Napster, a file-sharing service that made this underground activity accessible to anyone with an internet connection. In July 2001 the record industry succeeded in shutting Napster down, but it was too late. The contract between fans and the business – the tacit agreement about the 'worth' of a piece of music – had been broken. Many people found it laughable that they should go back to paying £13.99 for a CD. Luckily for them, they didn't have to, because three months after Napster ceased operations, Apple launched the first iPod.

If the idea of '1,000 songs in your pocket' wasn't life-changing enough, this digital jukebox had an extra setting: a randomised live mix of your music library. (Apple's 'shuffle' function was so popular that a few years later it launched a miniature version of the player that could do nothing else.) The iPod could be filled up by spending your evenings and weekends 'ripping' the CDs you already owned, transferring your illegally downloaded files or visiting the iTunes Store: a digital music warehouse with infinite aisles. Crucially, Apple's digital shop 'unbundled' albums: if you only wanted the two hits and none of the 'junk', to use Phil Spector's terminology, you could download your chosen songs for 79p each. There was very little financial incentive to purchase the full album.

In Apple's world, fans were buying individual tracks and shuffling them in one long, groovy, silhouetted party. The album was being stripped for parts. The idea horrified bands such as Radiohead, who refused to allow their music onto iTunes for several years before finally relenting in 2008. Since the Recording Industry Association of America began keeping count in 1973, albums – on vinyl, then cassette and CD – had always significantly outsold singles in the US. The download industry changed that dramatically: in 2012, 1.4 billion single digital tracks were sold, dwarfing album sales in all formats combined.[23]

The digital era was living up to the promise of Facebook's early motto, 'Move fast and break things'. Advances in technology meant that computers and portable devices were becoming faster and better connected: in 2007, Apple launched the first iPhone and more than half of UK households had broadband. Meanwhile, the word 'streaming' was making its way into the lexicon. In 2005, three former PayPal employees launched a video-sharing site called YouTube; the following year, two Swedish entrepreneurs founded a new 'audio streaming platform',

Spotify. By this time, the MP3 had all but killed the CD – but the download era was to be short-lived. Napster and iTunes had introduced the idea that there was no need to *physically* own music. With streaming, there was no need to own it at all.

The repercussions of this for the music industry have been enormous. With revenue from physical and digital sales falling, record labels and artists have little choice but to accept the paltry royalties offered by streaming services. In 2015 Geoff Barrow of the band Portishead shared his dismay at his total earnings for 34 million plays across Spotify, YouTube and Apple's streaming platform, Apple Music: just £1,700 after tax.[24] Thom Yorke criticised major labels for jumping into bed with Spotify 'because they see a way of re-selling all their old stuff for free, make a fortune, and not die'. Streaming was, he said, not the solution but 'the last desperate fart of a dying corpse'.[25] Touring, merchandise and licensing music to film and television have in many cases become more important to an artist's finances than making and selling albums.

Streaming, too, has further changed how we listen. Online interfaces are landscapes of distraction, with algorithm-driven suggestions at every turn: it requires a degree of resolve to commit to an album for its duration. Streaming services are sparing with the data they release, but a 2018 survey revealed that Americans spend 54 per cent of their listening time with individual tracks and only 18 per cent with albums.[26] On Spotify, neither the album nor the single is king: the playlist reigns supreme. Some artists are now tailoring their music to mood or genre-based playlists, from 'Massive Drum & Bass' to 'Sexy as Folk', 'Spooning' to 'Energetic Run'. They are avoiding long intros (if listeners grow impatient and skip your track, the algorithm downgrades it and your days are numbered), creating large quantities of music of a similar tempo and tone to keep listeners locked in (the most streamed artist of 2010 to 2020 was the Canadian rapper Drake, whose 2018 album *Scorpion* is an hour and a half long) and releasing multiple versions and collaborations to maximise their chances of being playlisted.[27] The rise of voice-recognition software such as Amazon's Alexa and Apple's Siri is likely to move us further towards listening by keyword.

*

It's deeply depressing to think that our complex relationship with music, our tangled strands of taste, emotion and memory, might be reduced to: 'Alexa, play sixties music' or 'Siri, play sad songs'. But it's easy to slip into alarmist thinking. Musicians may well be tweaking their work to suit new formats, but wasn't it always thus? Since pop music made its way onto the wireless in the sixties, long, noodling introductions have been avoided by bands in search of a radio hit. The jukebox introduced the 'shuffle' in the fifties; the cassette enabled mixtapes (proto-playlists) in the seventies and eighties. The album itself was a response to a format change, its playing time determined in the forties not by a vision of a new art form but by the desire to re-package Columbia Records' classical catalogue.

Not for the first time, reports of the album's demise have been greatly exaggerated. For musicians, it remains the ultimate vessel for their art. It's essential for both critical attention and commercial survival: playlists might get you on the Spotify payroll, but without an album it's harder to win awards, launch tours and sell T-shirts. There will always be someone mourning a lost golden age. But the Pulitzer Prize for music, which has been running since 1943, had never been awarded to a pop album until *DAMN.*, by the rapper Kendrick Lamar, won in 2018. And if you want an example of the density, craft, intelligence and urgency with which albums are still being made, *DAMN.* is a good place to start.

In the digital age, even 'pre-digital' artists have managed to use, rather than simply resist, the new technology. In 2007 Radiohead released their album *In Rainbows* as a pay-what-you-want download directly from their own site. It was a major event, and for me, downloading it – in a hotel room after a long day reporting on the Frankfurt Book Fair as a junior journalist at *The Times* – was just as exciting as queuing up for a CD of *Kid A* outside HMV at midnight seven years earlier as an undergraduate, having abandoned my Anglo-Saxon poetry for the night. The full impact of Beyoncé's *Lemonade* – a glorious album of black power and lover's retribution, released in 2016 on her own Tidal streaming platform – came from its sixty-five-minute digital film version. In 2019 Björk followed *Biophilia*, the first 'app album', with a virtual-reality version of her record *Vulnicura*, hosted online or as an interactive exhibition. At their extremes these developments might seem gimmicky (I like Björk's music too much to bother with her apps), but they are all noble attempts to recapture the excitement of an album's release and to preserve the intensity of the listening experience.

In search of that buzz (and crackle, hum and clunk), we are also returning to the humble LP. Since 2007, UK vinyl sales have increased by 2,000 per cent: in 2019, one in every eight albums bought was a vinyl record.[28] This is not pure retromania: alongside reissues of Fleetwood Mac and Joy Division in that year's vinyl top ten was a brand-new uncut gem of a pop record by a seventeen-year-old girl destined for great things – Billie Eilish. A Communist-era pressing plant in the Czech Republic, once destined to be a relic, now produces 24 million records a year.[29] Even the cassette – a convenience-driven format that is now highly inconvenient – is making a comeback. The tactile ritual involved in playing vinyl and tape; the warm, imperfect sound; the inability to shuffle – all these have a role in the revival of physical formats. There is an element of exhibitionism, too, in a music collection: it's a display of personality, of cultural capital, a way of making friends and lovers ('Come up and I'll show you my most-played Spotify tracks' doesn't quite cut it). It is an integral part of our identities, sometimes stubbornly so. My wife and I fell in love through a shared soundtrack – of Neil Sedaka, Arthur Lee, Morrissey and Motown. We have been together for nearly two decades and have two children. And yet, she still resists merging our vinyl collections – mainly, I think, because hers is bigger.

The revival of old formats might not be game-changing, but it is instructive. Though we can't dispute the fact that streaming is the future, we are not quite willing to jettison music's physical presence in our lives. And we are certainly not ready to say goodbye to the album.

In fact, for many, the opposite is true. Tired of the hyper-convenient but oddly unsatisfying experience offered by streaming platforms, listeners are returning to the album as an unbroken artwork: something with an emotional and sonic arc, to be played from start to finish without interruption. You might recall the thrill of the concerts in the 2000s in which artists from Brian Wilson to Sonic Youth would perform an album in its entirety; or you might have joined Tim Burgess's album-listening parties which began on Twitter during the coronavirus lockdowns of 2020; or you might, in a moment of nostalgia, simply have dusted off an old disc. But whether it's communal or solitary, via a vintage turntable or a smartphone, there is something revelatory about rescuing your favourite songs from the algorithm and placing them back where they belong. 'Here Comes the Sun' is an exceedingly pretty song – as I write, it is the Beatles' most-played track on Spotify. But it undergoes a strange alchemy when heard between the abruptly curtailed white noise of 'I Want You (She's So Heavy)' and the eight-miles-high harpsichord and harmonies of 'Because'. *Abbey Road* is more than the sum of its parts; it demands to be heard the way it was intended. All great albums do.

*

This book began life as a feature for the *New Statesman*, where I work. When I started approaching authors I admired to write about an album, I was keen that it shouldn't necessarily be their 'favourite', aware of the effect that word usually has on me: paralysis, panic, or a tendency to gravitate towards a safe, canonical choice. I asked instead for a 'cherished' album – one that is important to them, or had been important at a certain time. A record that changed them.

The pieces that came in showed just how deeply this form is embedded into our lives. Albums were Proustian madeleines that sent writers back to a time and place: Marlon James to a crisis of faith and sexuality in his twenties that was resolved by Björk's *Post*; Sabrina Mahfouz to a 5 a.m. rave in Ayia Napa, receiving an education in feminism from Ms. Dynamite; Eimear McBride to wandering home in the dark through Kentish Town to a soundtrack of the Tindersticks; Daljit Nagra to Sheffield where his family shop was defaced by racists who liked the same band as him.

It's perhaps unsurprising that many of the contributors chose albums that they first encountered in their teens. Adolescence is a time of heightened receptivity as well as emotional and sexual turbulence. Teenagers are deciding what sort of person they want to be, and music is one of the key inputs in that weird and unstable algorithm. For Deborah Levy, the effect of David Bowie's *Ziggy Stardust* was 'throwing petrol at the naked flame of teenage longing and desire for another sort of life'. When David Mitchell placed Joni Mitchell's *Blue* in his Walkman and strode home over the Malvern Hills the day after his last A level, its nakedness struck him with the force of revelation. As a fourteen-year-old in suburban St Louis, Patricia Lockwood found that Liz Fraser's voice left her 'motionless on the floor, gay, made of gauze, clutching myself against a background of dissolving stars'.

But these are not pure acts of nostalgia: the effects of life-changing albums are permanent and continuous. For Sarah Hall, Radiohead's *OK Computer* offers not a retreat into the past but 'a kind of amplification of the moment', an 'enhancement of life in real time'. Listening to Yes's album *Fragile* made George Saunders understand that 'to make something beautiful might mean to make something even you, the artist, don't fully understand' – the window that was 'thrown open' in his mind is open still.

Albums can alter the architecture of our minds. The ones that speak to us, we listen to hundreds of times over decades; we know them far better than any novel or film. They are faithful companions, with us from the first time we lower the needle to the last time we hover a thumb over the screen. They are, truly, long players.

Tom Gatti, 2020

Deborah Levy

The Rise and Fall of Ziggy Stardust and the Spiders from Mars by David Bowie (1972)

Bowie was ahead of everyone else (as usual) when he created a rock-star alter ego who was a citizen of Mars with the bonus of free movement to Earth. Ziggy Stardust (hair the colour of a blood orange, no eyebrows) died a long time before Bowie's final, sad farewell, but to be honest Ziggy is still wearing full make-up and is totally alive in my mind.

When I first got my hands on my very own copy of *The Rise and Fall of Ziggy Stardust and the Spiders from Mars*, its effect was nothing less than throwing petrol at the naked flame of teenage longing and desire for another sort of life.

I closed the door of my bedroom in West Finchley, north London, lit six joss sticks and placed them inside the glass milk bottles that I had been told to leave on the doorstep. Then I slipped the vinyl out of its vaguely *Blade Runner*-ish cover, lifted the needle of the record player and waited for the first throbbing, ominous drumbeats that announce the flamboyant drama of this crazed album.

Bowie's voice was as hysterical as I felt. He told me that I had five years left to cry in and that the earth was dying – which it still is. Despite the poetry and the despair, I was attracted to the glamorous line in 'Five Years' about glimpsing someone in an ice-cream parlour. Where could I find one in Finchley? Preferably open at midnight with Bowie sitting inside it. No doubt about it, Ziggy was going to lift me away from the suburbs into a glamorous, freakish, bigger world.

In the 1970s when girls were coerced into being the kind of girls that boys would apparently wish to marry, Ziggy Stardust messed gender all up. This was perfect because we were all messed up anyway. As for 'Rock 'n' Roll Suicide', Bowie's message was that I was not alone in my beautiful desolation, certainly not desperate enough to smoke my final cigarette and say goodbye to my older brother. He was listening to manly Bruce Springsteen in his bedroom while I sang along with Bowie's ooh la las, moped to 'Lady Stardust' and played 'Suffragette City' at full volume.

Above all, the delirium of Bowie's imaginative reach in his Ziggy Stardust era was an inspiration when I started to invent personas in my novels. In my view, Bowie was a great writer. He has influenced me more than Tolstoy ever will do. These days when I'm on a plane to Berlin, I put my headphones on and play Lotte Lenya singing 'Alabama Song' because Bowie sang it every morning when he lived in Berlin. And then I play 'Starman'. The cabin crew roll the trolley with its Pringles and mini bottles of gin down the aisle, and I think about how austerity Britain needs stardust and moonage daydreams so much more than it needs Brexit.

Clive James

Ellington at Newport by Duke Ellington (1956)

When I started at Sydney University in the late 1950s the first American jazz LPs were just coming in and I personally tested some of them to destruction on my Carrygram, which was set up in our kitchen at home. I had the Jelly Roll Morton and his Red Hot Peppers 12-inch LP, which I played until my mother rebelled after hearing 'The Chant' once or ten times too often. I also had a big Duke Ellington phase, centred around a sumptuous collection of the greatest hits of the 1940–1 band, although I didn't neglect the 10-inch LP of his hits from the early thirties, because my trumpet hero Rex Stewart was prominent in the line-up. But my most played Duke LP – I played it to death in fact, because the day came when it was too worn out to work at all – was the live recording from the 1956 Newport Jazz Festival at

31

which Duke's band tore the whole district to pieces with an extended version of 'Diminuendo and Crescendo in Blue'.

Boy, did I love that. I had never before rated Paul Gonsalves highly, but his tenor solo on that one went on and on beyond infinity and into the sublime. Listen to it now and you can hear how Duke's left hand was always the real driving force of the Ellington tempo. By now I've forgotten all the scholarship (was it Philly Joe Jones or just plain Jo Jones who was slapping the edge of the stage with a rolled-up newspaper as the hurtling melody climbed up and onward into a frenzy?). But if I get time I'll go back there and check up. Back to a time when Duke was alive.

I swapped smiles with him once, in the late sixties, after a Sacred Concert at Great St Mary's in Cambridge, but within seconds he was away in the car with the only side-man who was ever allowed to ride with him, Harry Carney; and I never saw him again, though I never stopped admiring the best of his music, either. Even when in the grip of grandiloquence, he would always swing, and in that Newport LP the whole orchestra swung like a train coming.

Patricia Lockwood

It'll End in Tears by This Mortal Coil (1984)

Full disclosure: I initially purchased this album for gay reasons. There's a sort of hot Pre-Raphaelite ghost clutching herself on the cover and I, a fourteen-year-old girl in suburban St Louis whose main cultural outlet was the local mall, found myself unable to resist her. Another disclosure: I did not, at the height of my musical listening career, listen to albums in a normal way. My usual practice was to lie down on the floor like a huge foetus, place my ear against the speaker, and pretend I was in a warm aural womb where God was growing me, through an umbilicus that could only be described as my own tenuous grip on reality. You might expect this attitude to prepare me to hear Liz Fraser's voice for the first time; it didn't.

No disrespect to the many other fine musicians who worked on this album, but for me it was about that voice – rooted, aerial, as flexible in its upper registers as it was rich in its middle, revolving around an unchanging axis of pitch, poured into various blown-glass containers of made-up language. It was like what a woman totally alone on a planet, unexposed either to other human beings or traditional forms of music, might decide to do with a nameless substance she had discovered in her own throat: play with it, stretch it, see what it could do. Toss it away, let it come back to her; teach it tricks, teach it words; drop it into a dry riverbed and let it flow uphill. *Was this what was going on in Scotland?*

I paused after her first song and experimentally hooted like a crystal owl. No, I couldn't do it. Harder than it looked. Impossible, actually. When the album was over, I uncurled myself from the speaker and sat up to examine the hot ghost on the jewel case, then flopped back down and pressed play again. Forgive the dramatics, but I had never been so completely the target audience for something before – motionless on the floor, gay, made of gauze, clutching myself against a background of dissolving stars, something valuable in my throat, I could feel it.

Lavinia Greenlaw

White Light/White Heat
by the Velvet Underground (1968)

I was hanging around my local record shop wondering what to listen to next. I'd made my way through punk assuming that because it seemed shapeless and rootless, it had come out of nowhere. I'd been young enough to believe this possible and had thrown out most of my records and clothes thinking that I could come out of nowhere too. Now music was revealing its connections the way art or poetry do when you've spent enough time inhabiting them. I relaxed, letting myself listen to soul again and talking about jazz without irony. I allowed that there was old stuff that was exciting, radical even. I was rummaging through the shop's second-hand section when among the Barclay James Harvest, Average White Band and 10cc, I found *White Light/White Heat*.

Recorded in 1968, it's the second Velvet Underground album and the last they made in their formative line-up. It's the most tense record I've ever heard and not one I play often. One minute it sounds like the most fabulous and finely judged convergence and the next as if the musicians belong to different bands and the tracks to different albums. It's an experiment in limits and scale. Every beautiful musical possibility is pushed out of shape or forced off the road, but the point is that the possibility was there in the first place. Each track contains elements of perfect pop: a solid chorus, a bouncy backing vocal, crisp riffs, express-train drumming, irresistible bass. Only we are given too little or too much, it's over too quickly or goes on too long.

The opening title track sets out as frayed rock and roll, over in a brisk three minutes, but it gets stuck in its own ending. Pop driven into a wall. This is followed by 'The Gift', three times as long: John Cale reading Lou Reed's short story in one speaker and music in the other. There I was, listening admiringly to an eight-minute rock instrumental as if punk had never happened.

Only there's nothing plodding and indulgent about this – or about 'Sister Ray', the album's wild but somehow catchy seventeen-minute finale. Musical surfaces form and shatter. There are distortions and perforations everywhere, and one moment of feedback so painful that it never gets any easier to take. On 'Lady Godiva's Operation', a ballad from the dark side, Reed overdubs certain vocal phrases as if he's leant over to shout them in your ear. The brief and delicate 'Here She Comes Now' is an idea of sweetness that refuses to progress.

I had never heard anything like *White Light/White Heat* and it changed how I listened as well as what I listened to next. It didn't come out of nowhere any more than punk did, but it couldn't have been made by a different line-up or even by the same people in a different place and time. It sounds no less original every time I hear it.

Marlon James

Post by Björk (1995)

Post caught me at a peculiar time in my life, right when life was the one thing I didn't want. Let's dismiss the two elephants in the room. I was not thinking of ending life, and *Post* didn't save it. The album did something deeper and richer. Here's the thing. Taking one's life is redundant if you're already at the end of yourself. That phrase I picked up in church, meaning that I, at the ripe old age of twenty-five, had run out of capital A answers to life's big questions. What is life? Why am I here? When does it stop hurting? Why do I like boys? Why doesn't Jesus like boys who like boys? *Post* didn't reply to any of these questions. Instead it gave answers to shit I didn't even ask.

It's cliché to say that a record sounds just a new as the first day one hears it. Except *Post*, and perhaps no other album (except Björk's own *Homogenic*), is so relentlessly present tense that every time sounds like the first time you're hearing it. Wide-eyed and childlike yet world-weary and aged, it creates a whole new present tense by smashing past and future together. And not just because it has both Tin Pan Alley and techno. Talking Heads did this too, but it never even occurred to me that I could live life this way. On my left, the past as garden of delights. On my right, the future as world of wonder. In the middle, a gloriously messy uncertainty.

But I wanted certainty, damn it. Uncertainty meant God was never going to play fortune teller and reassure me that my life was going to be normal, normal being the only measure of happiness. Uncertainty was not going to tell me that I would end up heterosexual (I didn't), or even make it out of my twenties alive (I did). *Post* pretty much said fuck that mess. Not knowing what's going to happen, and embracing both happiness and catastrophe as equally anticipatory outcomes, created an appreciation not of the outcome, but of the peace of mind to celebrate a future that could never be guaranteed.

'Possibly maybe,' she sang. But the real kicker was the line that followed. It started with 'probably', a million times more likely than possibly, if I remembered math class. And after that came a word that made me realise that there was one thing closer to certainty after all, a thing I never thought to expect, never thought I deserved.

Love.

Daisy Johnson

Cuz I Love You by Lizzo (2019)

When some friends and I first got tickets to Glastonbury in 2019 and I realised that Lizzo would be there, I listened to her album *Cuz I Love You* a lot in preparation. We listened on long car or train journeys, I put her on while walking or cooking, I played her to my family.

The temperature at Glastonbury skyrocketed, we sheltered in the shade, the toilets stunk, we queued at the water taps and for cold beer; still, we turned up to Lizzo early, dizzy, coated in glitter, caked with dust. There are moments that will always stay with you and seeing Lizzo that day is one of those for me. Her humility at being at Glastonbury was overwhelming, her performance was astounding. At one point on stage she says: 'I want you to know, if you can love me you can love yourself . . . We can save the world if we save ourselves first.'

After the festival we listened to the album even more. Often all together, in a kitchen in France on a writing retreat or in evenings in Oxford with the doors and windows of the house open, shrieking the words and getting a lot of them wrong, dancing inelegantly. The album became the soundtrack to a year that was both difficult and exciting in many ways. There were deaths in the family and a suicide attempt from a friend, my partner had just become self-employed and we were both working out how to make money from doing something that had previously only been a hobby. Holidays were not holidays, they were working trips. Lizzo's unique brand of self-love and her no-nonsense, sexy music were what I – and a lot of us – needed in 2019.

Cuz I Love You is a furious call for both self-sufficiency and universal care. Lizzo is capable of a soaring voice and a low, mesmeric rap. These songs are incantations, spells for better days. These are the songs you play when you are about to go into a meeting you are uncertain you belong in, or after a long day, walking home through the autumn dusk. They are joyful, raging, exuberant, at times funny and, in moments, incredibly meaningful. They are the songs I put on again, now, trying to write this piece, and they are, to me, as exciting as they were the first time around. When you hear them, it is only possible to dance.

Eimear McBride

Tindersticks by Tindersticks (1995)

The first time I heard this album was on the tape-of-a-tape
a friend gave me at drama school in 1995 – in the years
since, I've bought it many times over, in every format, so
my conscience is clear. I remember wandering home in
the dark through Kentish Town, north London, listening
to it on my Walkman and not really having any idea what
was going on. It was like nothing I'd heard before. From
the mercurial dissonance of its opener, 'El Diablo en el
Ojo', to the last delicate strains of 'Sleepy Song', I was in
its thrall and, many hundreds of listens later, that's how
I remain.

'Tiny Tears' is probably the album's most readily
recognisable track, from its outing in *The Sopranos*, but
I prefer the sorrowful poignancy of 'No More Affairs',
followed later on by what feels like a miniature, internal

trilogy: 'Cherry Blossoms', 'She's Gone' and 'Mistakes'. Picking out favourites feels like a transgression, though. The album's emotional cohesion is such a huge part of its pleasure that not listening from beginning to end, every time, is to risk missing the deeper submersion it offers.

There's a true, if disconcerting, magic to the three-way wedding of the album's beautiful, intricate scoring, the cigarette-stained, shame-filled intimacy of the lyrics and Stuart Staples's deep, dark, world-weary singing voice. The tension created between these elements produces songs that manage to be both epic and domestic all at once. For example, the third track, the spoken/sung 'My Sister', follows the story of the narrator's younger sister from their childhood pillow fights in which she'd wield a Stanley knife, to her temporary blindness, to causing the death of their mother – and cat – by smoking in bed, through the scandal of moving in at fifteen with a gym teacher, to becoming partially paralysed when, in a rage, he hits her over the neck with a Bullworker, finishing with her premature death at the age of thirty-two.

Bathos and tenderness are balanced throughout, from the heartbreak of the child – in her blindness, conjuring magical images – to the sighting of the teacher, released from jail, coaching a non-league football team in a Cornwall seaside town, to the brother's final assessment of why she wanted to be buried in a cheap coffin. It's a painful, wonderful song in which each facet adds up to create a whole, glimmering, tragic life. The merest hint of histrionics in either the delivery or the music beneath it would tip the song into farce and that never happens.

This album, the band's second – their excellent first album is also simply called *Tindersticks* – is the love of my musical life. I've listened to it incessantly since I was a teenager and I never grow tired of it. It has shaped how I think about life, love, men, sorrow and regret. It's a masterpiece and an undervalued one at that.

Billy Bragg

Ronnie Lane's Slim Chance by Ronnie Lane (1975)

After I left school in 1974, my social life consisted of playing rock and roll in various back rooms with my mates. When we felt we were good enough to do some recording, we scoured the classifieds in the back pages of *Melody Maker*, looking for studios. An ad for a place called Bearshanks Lodge, a converted farmhouse in Northamptonshire, offered a week's residential recording for a reasonable £150. We got in touch. The handwriting on the letter we got back had an air of familiarity: it looked very similar to that on the sleeve of *Ronnie Lane's Slim Chance*. Lane was a former member of the Faces, the band that provided much of the material for our sessions. He'd quit when Rod Stewart's solo pretensions began to overwhelm the integrity of the group.

The handwriting belonged to Jackie O'Lochlainn Mackay. It was her photograph of Ronnie Lane that adorned the front cover. The grainy, sepia-toned image is as earthy as a day spent walking the fields behind a one-horse plough. Lane stares into the camera, not quite smiling but with a mischievous look that tells you he doesn't take himself terribly seriously. It was his instinct for seeing through the glittery charade of early-seventies pop that ultimately led him to part company with the Faces and relocate to a farm in the Welsh Marches.

Jackie's husband, Ruan O'Lochlainn, was a member of the Slim Chance band, playing saxophone, piano and Hammond organ on the album. The photo within the gatefold sleeve shows him standing with the band against the crumbling masonry of what looks like an old barn wall. Lane is centre-stage, his long sideburns, drape coat and scarf giving him the look of the dodgy outsider in a Thomas Hardy novel who ultimately wins the day by pulling the squire from the mill pond or saving the sheep from some life-threatening predicament.

With mandolin, violin, accordion and Dobro guitar to the fore, this band, under Lane's direction, created something seldom heard in British pop. Taking cues from his post-war childhood, Lane drew on cowboy songs, pub singalongs and music-hall ballads as well as the likes of Chuck Berry, Fats Waller and the Mills Brothers. Throwing in half a dozen self-penned numbers, he built on a sound conceived in 'Lazy Sunday' and 'Itchycoo Park' to create an English country music that was neither traditional nor pastoral. The cover of Lane's first album had featured a picture of a rag-and-bone man on his horse and cart, and Ronnie lived up to that image, scouring the edgelands of British pop culture, carting off material that nobody wanted any more, utilising it to forge something new and beautiful.

Staying with Ruan and Jackie was like walking into the sleeve of one of our favourite records. They welcomed us in and their enthusiasm for our music gave us all a boost in confidence. Every time I hear Ruan's plaintive piano opening to 'Give Me a Penny', I find myself once again walking across the fields towards Bearshanks Lodge.

Teju Cole

Mos Def & Talib Kweli Are Black Star
by Black Star (1998)

By 1998, both Tupac and Biggie were dead. But hip hop was still alive, and a host of gifted MCs released albums that year: Wu-Tang Clan, Beastie Boys, Outkast, Jay-Z, DMX, Method Man. *The Miseducation of Lauryn Hill* came out in August, and in September *Mos Def & Talib Kweli Are Black Star* sent a shiver down the collective spinal cord. Or so I imagine: I wasn't really paying much attention at the time, my days consumed with a debilitating struggle against depression. I dodged classes and immersed myself in Ingmar Bergman films. It wasn't much of a solution, and I eventually dropped out of medical school, left Michigan, went to London for a year and came back to the US. When I returned in 2000, it was to New York. My first month back, I copped Mos

Def's *Black on Both Sides* at a record shop on Broadway near Columbia University. It gave me new ears, and led me to *Black Star*. I'm still listening.

Black Star was the only studio album of Black Star, the rap duo of Talib Kweli and Mos Def (now Yasiin Bey). But with such perfection, what need for a sequel? The album was track after track of pure poetry. But poetry is an elusive term: it means more than 'nice', obviously, but it also means more than work created primarily for the page. One could compare the prosody and rhythm of *Black Star* to Walt Whitman's 'Song of Myself' or to the poems of Langston Hughes. But the poetry of a great rap album cannot reside in its words alone, no matter how great (and *Black Star* is full of surpassingly great lines). Poetry, in the context of this album, is a question of breath, delivery and sonics, a mixture of modes that gives it precise kinship with its peers and forebears: MF Doom, Busta Rhymes, Rakim, the Jamaican dancehall artist Barrington Levy. *Black Star*'s allusions range as far afield as Bruce Lee's *Enter the Dragon* and Toni Morrison's *The Bluest Eye*. Poetry is technique manifested as affect.

Two decades pass, and I still cannot account precisely for why this is one of the albums of my life. It is permanently fresh and unflaggingly true. The clarity and velocity of Talib Kweli on 'Hater Players' remains unmatched. Mos Def's melancholy conjurations in 'Thieves in the Night' cast a spell. Both 'Definition' and 'Re: Definition' are pure pomp, while 'Respiration', my standout track in an album of standouts, seemed to encapsulate whatever gloom and hope I was feeling – young, black and male – in New York City in the first years of a new millennium. Propelled by spare and bass-heavy rhythms, this was music of the aftermath, but it was also suggestive of how things could be, its eloquence coursing through the lower frequencies like contraband thought.

The year is 1998. Mos Def and Talib Kweli, two of the finest Brooklyn MCs, with Hi-Tek on the decks, make lightning strike once – but once is more than enough.

Sandeep Parmar

Scarlet's Walk by Tori Amos (2002)

At 7 a.m. on 11 September 2001, I was awoken by a phone call from my father that was mostly incoherent panic. I was in Los Angeles, three hours behind New York City, and I was sleeping in the bed of a man I would not go on to marry. Planes; something else; come home. To Ventura, a sleepy suburb an hour north of Los Angeles, where I'd lived most of my life. That morning, the freeways in downtown were unusually empty. Cars stopped at traffic lights with their windows rolled down. Our radios blared talk. The days that followed were the start of wall-to-wall news coverage, a mainstay in the twenty-first century. About a week later, regular TV programming resumed.

I had been a Tori Amos fan since first hearing the track 'Winter' from her 1992 album *Little Earthquakes* on a Sony Walkman radio, hiding out in a closet while my parents argued. But when Amos covered Tom Waits's wistful song 'Time' on *The Late Show with David Letterman*, a week after 9/11, omitting the lines about boys splashing into the streets, I knew that the country I'd grown up in – as a British citizen with a lowly green card and a Californian twang – was forever changed. And that day changed us all: how we felt about being American and what being an American meant. We singled out the 'sleeper' enemy within, and, for the first time in my living memory, we did it in a way that was racially identifiable. By the time I moved back to England in 2002, privileged to travel freely across the world, America became another lost homeland in a familial thread of immigrant losses from India's Partition onwards.

Amos's 2002 album *Scarlet's Walk* is an imagined post-9/11 journey from California ('the Ventura', colloquial for the 101 Freeway, appears in 'A Sorta Fairytale') to the East Coast. The album narrates an American landscape riddled with suppressed voices, seedy flirtations, crisis and injustice. Its female figure of Scarlet traces a lost America, a nation that would turn on itself, pointing madly at people like me and my brown family. (Our neighbours asked why we didn't plant an American flag in our front lawn.)

Amos's compassion and revulsion for what America had become or more likely had always been – a land celebrating immigrants alongside a foundational violence against otherness – spoke to me deeply. The daughter of a Methodist minister, Amos is also part Cherokee: her song 'Wampum Prayer' points to the genocide of Native peoples underpinning an ideological project by the founding fathers to rival all nations. 'I Can't See New York' and 'Pancake' address the World Trade Center attacks directly while balancing individual vulnerability with historical hypocrisies.

I was in NYC three days before the attacks and a boy I didn't really like invited me to tour the twin towers with him. I refused. I did not know then its fated significance as a vantage point over the previous century, nor could I have imagined the loss of so many lives to come at home and in the misguided War on Terror. The album's closing track, 'Gold Dust', is an elegy for lost innocence, orchestra and vocals dipping to a whisper over the base of Amos's signature Bösendorfer piano. Her album is a reminder of mourning. Not for the many who died, but for a country to which no one – myself included – can ever return.

Kate Mossman

The Rhythm of the Saints by Paul Simon (1990)

When I was ten, we entered a raffle at an ice rink and won a holiday to the south of France. The holiday was actually a week in a four-berth caravan, and transport to France was not included in the prize, but it was the most exciting thing that had happened to the family. The mountains of the Massif de l'Esterel, thirty miles from Nice, were red volcanoes. The trees were black from spontaneous fires. The hot air vibrated in a permanent mirage and our clothes dried within seconds of throwing ourselves into the springs of the national park. For that week, and the three-day drives on either side of it, we had one soundtrack: the album Paul Simon made after *Graceland*.

This was Simon's Latin American project. It features around a hundred musicians, from Puerto Rico to Brazil.

It went multi-platinum in the UK, but it had no hit singles. He once played it to nearly a million people in Central Park, but critics rarely talk about it now.

The scale and ambition of the record slip by unnoticed, because *The Rhythm of the Saints* just floats. Simon started with the drums – whole battalions of them, recorded live on the streets of Salvador – and built everything else on top. It has the highest concentration of exquisite melodies I've ever heard in one work of music. And it teems with lines of iridescent poetry. Lime-green lizards scuttle down cabin walls. 'Song dogs' bark at the break of dawn; streets are quiet as a sleeping army.

Listening is a tropical experience but the locations are scattered: a little harbour church of St Cecilia, a river as wide as the sea. Liberated from the political charge of *Graceland*, Simon instead focuses on the passionate realities of being human. He catches the contradictions of middle age – anxiety versus don't-give-a-damn confidence; irritation versus the broader sense of beauty that getting older allows. He looks at marriage with tender ambivalence and at old age with fear, evoking a shadow in the family, or a baby waving bye-bye. Images like these made me sad as a child, but they made me intrigued about the future, too.

The Rhythm of the Saints is a multi-sensory experience, a kind of musical synaesthesia. It actually *sounds* hot. It will forever be associated, for me, with the trip to that strange burning French moonscape: we were listening to the euphoric 'Proof' when we cleared a mountain bend and got caught in a herd of wild boar; to us children, their snouts became the horn section.

Simon's vivid but self-conscious focus upon beauty, and upon the moment, was something I later found in the poetry of the Caribbean writer Derek Walcott. Reading up on *The Rhythm of the Saints*, I realised that Walcott inspired the whole album. Simon would sing his poetry over tracks when he hadn't finished his own lyrics. Here were two difficult artists whose work was the easiest outlet for expressions of love or light. They did a musical together once – *The Capeman* – and it bombed.

George Saunders

Fragile by Yes (1971)

The artistic impulse first reared its head in the form of a relation to the Catholic Mass. The Mass taught me what a metaphor was and that there were notions deeper than words could express, and that a grand design could be manifest in the smallest detail. Each Mass had an ethos, a stance. A colour scheme could represent a particular aspect of God. Here was God sorrowful (purple, lamb-dominated), here God joyful (sun and angels, yellow and gold). Then adolescence came and the artistic impulse found a new repository: rock albums. Each album was a Mass of sorts, conveying meaning in its every particular.

A favourite of mine from that period was Yes's *Fragile*. It looked different from other albums. It had a gorgeous and strange Roger Dean painting on the front (the abundant Earth, cracking open) and was lush in its interior presentation. The music struck me as a precise, exuberant chaos, little trace in it of the blues-rock musical basis through which I (a beginning guitarist) was understanding everything at that point.

I was particularly taken by Steve Howe: he relied on almost no effects, played with extraordinary heart and precision, and – if memory serves – there was a photo of him smiling sweetly, standing among some sheep. I found it encouraging to think that someone happy could be as wonderful a player as he was. The lyrics were odd and poetic, as if the goal was to sound a certain way rather than to say a certain something. 'In and around the lake/ Mountains come out of the sky and they stand there.' *Yes, they do, sort of, don't they?* thought my 1974 self.

I was no artist at that point but badly wanted to become one. Yes reached across the Atlantic and tweaked something in my mind. I could find no overt 'meaning' in *Fragile* – except for the intensity of the experience I had listening to it. I couldn't deny what was happening to me but couldn't explain it or reduce it to thematics. It was just beautiful (confounding, grand, propulsive). Did Yes know the 'meaning' of *Fragile*? I suspected not. And yet . . . it meant.

So, a window was thrown open in my mind: to make something beautiful might mean to make something even you, the artist, don't fully understand. An artist may not, as she creates the work, have her aim fully worked out. The aim is realised through the process of making, and an aim realised through the making is going to be more profound than an aim decided upon in advance. ('Finding by doing' is how the director Hiro Murai once described this process to me.)

I listened to *Fragile* recently and found it as fresh as ever: startling, brash, complex, refusing to succumb to tropes or settle into any recognisable genre, still thrilling, still speaking to me after all these years.

Bravo, Yes, and, from the kid I was back then, thanks.

Preti Taneja

Midnight Marauders by A Tribe Called Quest (1993)

Midnight Marauders came out in 1993. Back then, all the boys I knew were into their dad's Pink Floyd or Dire Straits records. There was one who listened over and over to *Brothers in Arms*; it made him cry, he said, because he couldn't sign up. He signed on instead, like most of them did – or they worked in temp jobs while the older girls at my school rolled their skirts up at the waist and went down town in the lunch hour to smoke Marlboro Lights in the cafe above John Menzies. Brown girls seeking escape: where could we get it in our small towns? An Auntiji would call our mothers before we could even get home. They were the kind ladies of the corner shop and local bra factory; they knew me. I was the quiet girl, squashed into her coat, always silent in a crowd.

There was an Our Price in the arcade near the indoor sabji market; I would slip inside and listen to music with headphones on. That must be how I found A Tribe Called Quest: the beats relentless, the words knowing, the sound warm and smooth.

And though I could hear echoes of my early years, through the ask and response and the vocal control (the breath-held pauses sounded akin to the kirtans the Aunties sang at home), outside my window were whispering trees and muddy lanes. The church. The pub. The pond. School. Inside my head there were problems, in my bedroom there were problems; downstairs there were problems and we lived at the junction of two dead ends. Phife Dawg, Ali Shaheed Muhammad and Q-Tip sang about having problems, but they were not my problems: their hip hop and problems were my escape.

I had a bright-yellow Sony Walkman and I'd play it into the night. Staring at the plaster stippling on my ceiling, I fell for the promise in their sound. It was euphoric with language in a way most school poetry locked out. I learned lists, internal rhyme, stream of consciousness, politics, register, truth, tone, point of view and the proud articulation of identity as I had never encountered it before (except in my mother, dancing). Those were the years when the local boys' motto was *Don't drink and drive, smoke and fly*. The pale girls circled around them, dressing as Madonna, borrowing bindis and bangles and mehndi, which they called 'henna tattoo'. I gave up my treasures too willingly and kept quiet, listening to my tapes at home.

No one knew I was searching to lose something of myself; no one knew my disguises and what I was learning to steal. Between my ears there was the fresh mix of samples, the trumpet for punctuation. I shed skins to that music and grew gills and scales. In my mind I became my own tribe. It was midnight and I went marauding.

John Harris

A Love Supreme by John Coltrane (1965)

It must have been early 1987. BBC2 had just broadcast a feature-length documentary about Jack Kerouac, which, thanks to curiosity and the knowledge that Bob Dylan was in it, I had taped on to a VHS. By the following week, I had got hold of *On the Road* and joyously sped through it. But before that, I repeatedly played the part of the film dedicated to Kerouac's musical tastes, and his elegy to Charlie Parker, whose expression was as 'calm, beautiful and profound' as Buddha.

With my sixth-form friend Neil, I decided that now was the time to go beyond indie-rock and hip hop and sample the higher pleasures of jazz. This involved two places: a cut-price vinyl outlet in the backstreets of Manchester where I got two Parker records for £3 a piece and a Dizzy Gillespie one for even less; and the library in my hometown of Cheshire, where one album now screamed out to be borrowed. Probably via the *NME*, I already had some vague notion of John Coltrane's *A Love Supreme* – released in January 1965, and arguably the composer and sax player's greatest achievement – as a totem of cool, but the Kerouac connection made it feel obligatory. It was 25p for a two-week loan, plus a quid for a TDK C90 tape: a no-brainer, as we didn't say back then.

Then came another epiphany. This was the most transcendent music I had ever heard. Coltrane's sleeve notes, which refer to a 'spiritual awakening' he experienced in 1957 ('This album is a humble offering to Him . . . An attempt to say "THANK YOU GOD" through our work, even as we do in our hearts and with our tongues'), must have helped put me in the right mood, but what I divined in the music came to mind with no prompts. This opening mixture of the album's central four-note motif and McCoy Tyner's questing piano chords seemed to evoke the night, and rain; the sax part that awakened the track titled 'Resolution' after twenty seconds sounded like a sudden dawn; in between, the passage in which Coltrane intoned the title as a mantra was full of a power I couldn't even begin to articulate. This was heady, elemental stuff.

At Neil's house, where we spent whole Saturdays immersed in music and eating Lancashire cheese toasties, it worked the same magic; at night, when I would play it on the Binatone cassette player next to my bed, it entranced me even more.

It still does. I feel it as keenly in my fifties as I did when I was seventeen. When the world seems to be reducible to trivia, nastiness and a lack of hope, *A Love Supreme* gets as close to attesting to a higher power as any record ever has, and seems to offer an eternal assurance: that, on some elevated plane accessible only when the right music plays, all is well.

Meg Rosoff

This Year's Model by Elvis Costello (1978)

Genesis? Aerosmith? Steely Dan? No wonder I hated 1976. I moved to London in 1977 – twenty years old and desperate to escape Boston. My mentor, the sculptor Dimitri Hadzi (who had no more idea what he was doing at Harvard than I did), suggested art school. 'They're all stiffs here,' he said. Within a week of arriving at St Martins I found myself at the Live Stiffs Tour: Elvis Costello, Nick Lowe, Ian Dury & the Blockheads. It felt like a bomb going off in my head. Weird, smart lyrics; heavy percussion; rough, tough sound. Two thousand people got up and danced to 'Sex & Drugs & Rock & Roll'.

In 1979, I returned to Boston, finished my degree, moved to NYC and took a series of grim, low-paid jobs. A guitarist friend lent me his 1968 Fender Telecaster Bass. If Tina Weymouth can do it, he said, so can you. I practised for hours in my fifth-floor tenement apartment on Christopher Street, learning bass lines from the Clash, Television, Talking Heads. Some were impossible to follow (Ian Dury's bass player, Norman Watt-Roy, was hopelessly out of my league), but Bruce Thomas on *This Year's Model* was perfect.

I started with 'Pump It Up' and '(I Don't Want to Go to) Chelsea', moved on to the mad runs of 'Lipstick Vogue' and 'The Beat'. Costello was my first rock-and-roll god, but Thomas was all seven archangels at God's right hand. I probably played that album ten thousand times. No one ever suggested I quit my day job, but the band wasn't too bad, and we played at CBGB once. It was the antidote to my entire life so far.

Sarah Perry

Rachmaninov's *Piano Concertos Nos 2 and 4*
performed by Sequeira Costa (1993)

There was never any pop or rock music in the house
when I grew up, so the idea of an album in the ordinary
sense (parents playing the Beatles in the car; saving up for
your first record and then, later, wearing a band T-shirt;
whatever is the usual way of things) means very little to
me. The first album I got for myself was a free CD taped
to the front of a BBC music magazine, *The Best of Chuck
Berry*. I suspect I only very dimly realised the music was
from decades before.

So my favourite album, I'm afraid, is the Portuguese
pianist Sequeira Costa's recording of Rachmaninov's
second piano concerto. My father is a great fan of classical
music, and he had a pair of enormous mahogany-
veneered speakers that towered over me when I was a

small child, and shivered when he played the Beethoven Late String Quartets at top volume. One morning – I think I was about thirteen, which is exactly the age of sentiment and yearning when you ought, ideally, to first encounter Rachmaninov – I was coming down the stairs, and as I reached the landing the opening chords rang out through the house. I was so thunderstruck I sat on the steps to listen, and by the end of the first movement I was in tears.

I wafted into the room and declared that it was my favourite piece of music, ever, and that I would never listen to anything else. I had no idea, of course, that it's largely considered too sentimental for words, and good for nothing but films in which people swoon at each other on railway station platforms – as far as I was aware, it was a rare and splendid discovery and one that I needn't share with anybody else.

Since then I have listened to it over and over again, always leaping to my feet as the first movement goes into its transports of ecstasy, then sinking back into melancholy in the second movement. Costa's recording isn't, so far as I know, especially admired or well known, but for me it is the standard from which every other pianist deviates. Every other performance I've heard is too hasty, too bright in the opening chord progression; only Costa gets it right – only Costa makes me feel thirteen again.

Neil Tennant

The Man-Machine by Kraftwerk (1978)

With *The Man-Machine*, Kraftwerk made experimental German electronic art music the sound of pop. They'd had a novelty hit in 1975 with 'Autobahn', but their evolving exploration of difficult synthesiser technology was appreciated by a growing cognoscenti, David Bowie in particular paying close attention as *Radio-Activity* was followed by *Trans-Europe Express*.

Electronic music was happening. Giorgio Moroder's astonishing productions for Donna Summer took the brutal power of sequenced electronic music and made it erotic and hugely commercial; soon Patrick Cowley would do the same for gay dance music. Kraftwerk were intellectual electronic perfectionists but had an underrated gift for simple melodies attached to minimalist, modernist lyrics, somehow both bleak and romantic. A cool contemporary pessimism was expressed together with the promise of a robotic and technology-driven future in which lay the seeds of a new and ever-cooler pessimism.

It was irresistible. I remember sitting with friends on a Saturday night in a basement flat in Kilburn listening to this album the week it was released. We were all aware that it was something special and new. Night in the city had never been more poignant with its 'shimmering neon lights'. Alienation was glamorous and you could dance to it. Computer love was just around the corner.

Soon Kraftwerk would inspire huge pop hits from the likes of the Human League, OMD and Visage, and in the process find themselves the sound of the zeitgeist. In 1982 a song from *The Man-Machine* hit number one. 'The Model' was made in the seventies, a hit in the eighties, and its cold, ironic glamour still resonates today. In 1978 I wanted to live in this album.

Melissa Harrison

Movements by Booka Shade (2006)

I don't want to listen to it. I've swept the worn brick floor of the 300-year-old cottage I moved into just a month ago, brought in some firewood and cleaned the kitchen in an attempt to put it off. At last I get my laptop out – and spend an hour browsing vintage light fittings. I don't turn on my Bluetooth speaker; I don't open Spotify. I really don't want to listen to it, this album that has meant so much to me for so long.

Dance music has been my great love since I first went to the legendary Club UK in 1993, when I was just eighteen. It changed my life, as so many lives were changed by something that – it's easy to forget – was a countercultural revolution, one that sparked feelings of community and loyalty unimaginable now that the secretive world of what was once called 'clubbing' is big business, and completely mainstream. But as dance music has grown and changed, I've remained within it rather than outgrowing it; as well as being a nature writer and novelist I worked from 2006 to 2020 at *Mixmag*, the world's biggest club culture magazine.

When Booka Shade's *Movements* came out I was thirty-one and still going out at least a couple of times a month, as well as spending time in Ibiza every year. Just as important as clubs – perhaps more so – were afterparties, the chemically assisted, 'all back to mine' sessions that stretched on well into the next day, and sometimes the following night. Soundtracking the 'afters' was a fine art; it had to be electronic, of course, but often what was required was something more restrained, more contemplative than the bangers you'd spent seven hours dancing to in the club. There was room for emotions more subtle than euphoria, too; for nostalgia, or gentle melancholy even, as the sun came up and you pulled the blinds down and racked everyone out another line.

Movements was among an arsenal of albums and DJ mixes that fitted the bill, and I'd find it hard to listen to any of them now without an acute rush of feelings linked to the very particular atmosphere my friends and I built at those afterparties: intense, collusive and hedonistic, deeply trusting and connected, but addictively, dizzyingly separate from the world. The second album from Frankfurt's Walter Merziger and Arno Kammermeier, *Movements* was an early sign of a slow shift in dance music towards experimental, ambient and neoclassical, a shift that eventually gave us Nils Frahm, Max Richter, Kiasmos and many more. The album's high-point, for me, remains the sparse but driving 'In White Rooms', a track that works equally as well on the dancefloor as it does on headphones, and which remains just as emotive and hypnotic all these years on as the day it was made.

Often, at afterparties, we'd take down all the clocks, even taping over those on ovens or microwaves. We wanted to exist outside of time with one another, safe from our jobs, our families, our responsibilities; and we succeeded, for a while. But, of course, it couldn't last, and *Movements* proved more than just a shift towards what was arguably a more mature kind of dance music; it was also the beginning of the end of my own much-prolonged adolescence.

Colm Tóibín

Give a Damn by the Johnstons (1969)

The Johnstons began as an Irish folk band with a brother and two sisters, the sisters doing close harmony. When the brother left, two of Ireland's most formidable musicians and singers joined – Paul Brady and Mick Moloney. The band signed on the Transatlantic label and released two albums on the same day in 1969. I was fourteen and generally could not afford LPs but, after a visit from a generous aunt, I had enough money to buy *Give a Damn*, the album with more contemporary songs, and I played it over and over until I wore it out.

Adrienne and Lucy Johnston could do extraordinary harmonies: Adrienne's voice was deeper, Lucy's frailer and sweeter. They created an effect that was both sharply confident and yet left a shivering aftersound. I had not heard much Leonard Cohen, Jacques Brel or Joni

Mitchell when I bought the album. The band's version of 'Both Sides Now' was almost a pop song. The sisters sang it fast and in harmony. With Mitchell's 'Urge for Going', on the other hand, they used a low-key orchestral arrangement, with more horns than strings, and worked on the sheer loneliness of the song, as they would later with Mitchell's 'Marcie'.

Alone, in the front room of a small house on the edge of a town in the south-east of Ireland, I imagined the world courtesy of these songs. Four decades later, at a concert one night in Charlottesville in the United States, I found that Mick Moloney was sitting behind me. When a song called 'Sweet Thames Flow Softly' began, I turned around and said: 'You recorded that with the Johnstons!' But I couldn't explain to him how closely I had examined the photos on the album sleeve in 1969, or how attentively I had listened when the two men in the band entered the harmony, or had moments singing alone, or in one case when they sang a whole song without the sisters – Jacques Brel's 'Amsterdam'.

The highlight of the album for me was Adrienne singing 'Hey, That's No Way to Say Goodbye', with a very subtle guitar accompaniment that stayed under the vocal line, and the others coming in each time to do harmony on the last line. Maybe it mattered that Adrienne didn't try an American accent, but I think it mattered more that all four members of the band came out of an Irish tradition where the song was more important than the singer and the singer was encouraged to sing without any accompaniment, especially if the song was sad. The Johnstons didn't make Leonard Cohen's song sound like an Irish ballad: it had a fully modern sound; but there was rawness in the way the words were sung, a rawness that mattered to me in that room when I was a teenager. Many years later, I tried to write about a band like the Johnstons in a story called 'Famous Blue Raincoat'.

It was presumed, if you read about the band then, that they were destined for the same fame as won by Steeleye Span and Pentangle, but after *Give a Damn* Lucy left the Johnstons, and in 1971 Mick Moloney departed as well. Adrienne Johnston died in 1981. After *Give a Damn*, they recorded some good songs, including a plaintive version of Cohen's 'Story of Isaac' and some wonderful Irish traditional material. But that album was, for me, their high-point.

Bernardine Evaristo

Selections 1976–1988
by Sweet Honey in the Rock (1997)

I first heard Sweet Honey in the Rock sing at the 1985 UN
World Conference on Women in Kenya, where they blew
me away. It was my first visit to Africa and I was a young
black feminist surrounded by 13,000 feminist women
from all over the world, many in traditional dress. It was
an incredible and unforgettable experience, and Sweet
Honey gave the triumphant closing concert in Nairobi.
They are an African American, female a cappella group
whose vocal power and range would put some of today's
biggest singers, who rely on autotune, to shame. Their
rousing and political songs, which veer from themes
of injustice and oppression to expressions of love and
beauty, are steeped in the traditions of blues, soul, gospel,
folk and reggae.

I subsequently saw them appear every time they gave a concert in London, the audiences primarily packed out with women. More than twenty women have come and gone since the group was formed in 1973, and I like to think I caught them in their heyday during the eighties. If one group encapsulates the early years of black feminism, it's this one. They've earned several Grammy nominations, including for best contemporary folk recording, although that doesn't do justice to the variety of their music styles.

I've chosen *Selections 1976–1988* because it introduces people to some of their best songs. Sometimes I go years without listening to them, and then I'm driving along somewhere, put this album into the CD player and I'm immediately and sublimely transported – emotionally, intellectually, spiritually.

Jonathan Coe

A Symphony of Amaranths by Neil Ardley (1972)

It was in the late 1970s, on a visit to the wonderful record section at Birmingham's (now sadly demolished) Central Library, that I discovered this album. And ever since then, I've been obsessed with this question: how can one of the most diverse, inventive and beautiful records ever made in Britain remain so little known?

Neil Ardley is one of the forgotten geniuses of British music. He was a central figure to that thriving, close-knit community of musicians who did so much to enliven the British jazz scene of the late 1960s and early 1970s: names such as Ian Carr, Don Rendell, Mike Gibbs, Jon Hiseman and Barbara Thompson. Central to this movement was Ardley's New Jazz Orchestra, which provided a vehicle not just for playing but for long-form, ambitious composition. Ardley's works grew more and more expansive during this time, starting with the lovely miniature *Le Déjeuner sur l'Herbe* and culminating in this epic but still intimate work, recorded in 1971 under the supervision of the visionary producer Denis Preston.

Side one contains the 'Symphony'. There are four movements: Carillon, Nocturne, Entracte and Impromptu. The titles hint at classical music and you can tell that this is where Ardley's ambitions were starting to take him. There is a strong Gil Evans influence, but Ardley pushes the jazz orchestra's palette further by including strings, woodwinds, harp and tuned percussion. The textures are sometimes bold and brassy, but just as often featherweight and delicate: modal harmonies summon up an English pastoral feel that recalls Vaughan Williams more than Duke Ellington. The soloing – particularly from Ian Carr – is sublime.

Side two is full of further delicious surprises. There is a ten-minute setting of Edward Lear's 'The Dong with a Luminous Nose', narrated by Ivor Cutler with lugubrious glee. And then three exquisite songs to words by W. B. Yeats, James Joyce and Lewis Carroll, with Norma Winstone's voice sounding even more honeyed and crystalline than usual. The first of these – Yeats's 'After Long Silence', with its subtle woodwind flavourings, autumnal tonalities and eloquent tenor solo from Don Rendell – is a true masterpiece.

It's rare to find any album one can listen to hundreds of times without ever tiring of it. This, for me, is one of that special breed – and not just because it always gives me a nostalgic pang to remember the lucky day I chanced upon it in a Birmingham library.

Alan Johnson

Revolver by the Beatles (1966)

The album wasn't a recognisable art form, or even a particularly desirable acquisition among music fans, before the Beatles. Elvis consigned his dreadful film scores to 33⅓ vinyl, but by the time the Fab Four came along 'The King' had been managed into musical senility. If the British pop stars of the time – Cliff, Billy, Marty or Adam – released an LP, it was to earn extra royalties from their regurgitated singles. When, in February 1964, Cathy McGowan broke the news on *Ready, Steady, Go!* that the Beatles had reached number one in the US charts, a feat that seemed to me as amazing as the conquest of Everest, her teenage audience knew that 'I Want to Hold Your Hand' wasn't destined to be reproduced as an album track. For UK followers, the Beatles could be relied upon to invariably provide only new music for the extra outlay required to buy an LP.

Their albums always contained gems that were thrillers rather than fillers, from 'I Saw Her Standing There' through 'All My Loving' and 'I Should Have Known Better' to 'Yesterday'. Then came the rhapsodic phase when every new record seemed designed to take the pop album to a new and previously unobtainable level. Sandwiched between *Rubber Soul* and *Sgt. Pepper's Lonely Hearts Club Band* in this amazing trilogy was *Revolver*. When it was released in the summer of 1966, I was working at Tesco on Hammersmith's King Street where the man who delivered the Nevill's bread at 8.30 every morning also carried a stock of contraband EMI albums, which he sold at half price.

It was from Fred the bread man that I acquired the musical highlight of that or any other summer. (I like to think there was an egg man somewhere destined to carry knocked-off copies of *Magical Mystery Tour*.) The title's clever pun enshrined the way we listened to music at the time (and are increasingly doing so again): putting a slab of vinyl the size of a large pizza onto a turntable, applying the needle and listening as it moved through the five or six tracks on that side before turning it over to complete the process.

What glorious music emerged from *Revolver*, the first fruits of the Beatles' decision to concentrate on the studio rather than the stage. Familiarity has made it impossible to recapture the initial impact of tracks such as 'Eleanor Rigby', 'And Your Bird Can Sing', 'Got to Get You Into My Life' or 'Tomorrow Never Knows'. On one album they demonstrated their complete mastery of every rock music genre from R&B to psychedelia. For me, and I suspect millions of others, it remains the greatest testament to the incredible musical and cultural phenomenon that was the Beatles.

Will Harris

Regulate . . . G Funk Era by Warren G (1994)

It's hard to think about music without thinking of my dad. Dad making me sit through the eight-minute album version of Donna Summer's 'I Feel Love'. Dad coming home with numerous plastic bags (or boxes) of LPs, my mum screaming at him from the kitchen. Dad when he became obsessed with Bootsy Collins or Shania Twain or Leonard Nimoy or 'Hello Muddah, Hello Fadduh (A Letter From Camp)'. His passions have always been so broad as to obliterate any concept of taste. But there were two genres he managed to leave untouched: jazz and rap. So in my teens that's what I listened to.

I was probably about fourteen when I bought a CD of Warren G's *Regulate . . . G Funk Era* from the Music & Video Exchange in Notting Hill, while my dad browsed through the record section. That was also where I bought albums by Tha Dogg Pound, Dr. Dre, Tupac and others from Death Row Records' mid-nineties stable.

I had a feeling I should have been more into East Coast rap. It was faster, darker and more serious. And there were albums I loved, like GZA's *Liquid Swords*, which drew on the East in a way that – to an East Asian-looking teenager – was exciting and discomfiting. But I kept drifting back West. In California, the tempo was slower, the bass funkier, and Nate Dogg could be heard cooing in the background like a stock dove whose tongue had been coated in honey and pancake batter.

Listening to those albums again, it can't be a coincidence that GZA sampled dialogue from *Shogun Assassin*, while Warren G turned to *Young Guns*, the 1988 Western starring Charlie Sheen. Fantasy versions of East and West bolstered their differences. And maybe there's some kind of analogy to be drawn with how I felt as a teenager, caught between warring versions of my mum's Indonesia and my dad's England.

But I didn't listen to *Regulate* – or anything else – to make sense of things. In fact, I've always been a bad listener. I forget lyrics and mangle tunes. I also grew up in Hammersmith, a world away from Long Beach. As Warren G was rapping about throwing dice, flexing steel and gang-banging, I was shouting at my dad to stop playing a sitar cover of 'While My Guitar Gently Weeps' so I could do my homework.

G-funk had a philosophy: rhythm was life and life was rhythm. Warren G says he got that line from the rapper Jimmy Spicer, but I think there's a long tradition – linking rap and poetry – that would argue similarly. It comes from a sense that rhythm is both inadequate to life and much more than it. Rhythm exceeds what can be said; it transcends material hardship and brings that hardship into relief. But in the moment of flow, everything becomes synonymous. It's a philosophy you feel in your toes, an aporia in which sound and self dissolve and become briefly one whole. Which is to say, you can only understand it while you're listening to it.

Bonnie Greer

Cheap Thrills by Big Brother and
the Holding Company (1968)

Everyone has a time when childhood ends and this thing
called 'on your own' begins. This time was the summer
of 1968, not long after the assassination of Martin Luther
King, and it was my gap year before beginning university.
I was the eldest child of two people who worked hard to
better the lives of all of us kids. And being two African
Americans whose origins were in the South, our parents
wanted to have a safe and 'proper' life. We were raised
carefully, shielded against the various pitfalls, accidents
of society and flotsam and jetsam of African American
life. Our little house, with its neatly cultivated lawn in
front and garden in the back, its two-car garage and
swept front steps, was the replica of all of the houses
in our street. Church on Sundays, school uniforms, no

blaring music – all of this was to help us be the opposite of what society assumed about us.

In my case this was all going to plan until the year 1968 arrived. A series of national catastrophes and opportunities presented themselves, and I seized the moment and flew away. One of my landing places was the campus of the University of Chicago where a friend was an undergrad. One afternoon, I saw an album lying on a bed. It was called *Cheap Thrills* by something called Big Brother and the Holding Company. Its cover was a lurid cartoon landscape, and the record itself provided the leitmotif for the life I was about to live.

I was a black girl from the South Side of Chicago. The blues was part of my DNA. The blues was in the speaking voices of the old people. You could hear it coming out of houses on Sunday afternoon, usually low and furtive. It was on the radio. It was everywhere. It was *our* music, so how could a white girl from Texas sing it? In those days I was too green to know the answer to that. I waited for something derivative to appear, some phony sound to come out of the mouth of this Texan called Janis Joplin. But that never happened.

She sang 'Summertime' like she invented the song herself, and 'Ball and Chain' like she lived that life all the time. That is all that singing the blues requires. Hers was a jaunty and reckless existence and you could hear the bourbon in her veins. Joplin did not clean up the blues, nor hide it, nor give it permission to be. When later I heard that she had found Bessie Smith's unmarked grave and given it a headstone, I was not surprised. *Cheap Thrills* is about being a woman on the open road, taking what comes and living to tell the tale.

That afternoon of my epiphany, I played it about five times in succession. On the fifth playing, I knew that it was embedded. I didn't need to hear it ever again. I had my orders.

David Mitchell

Blue by Joni Mitchell (1971)

In that shadowy era before the internet, buying an LP on spec was a risky venture. Your only means of hearing an album before handing over your non-refundable £5.49 was by listening to someone else's copy – in which case you could just tape it. Printed reviews came and went at the speed of discarded magazines, and DJs' opinions were available only in real time. No podcasts, no archives, no nothing. For old releases, all you could do was try to divine the quality of the material from cover art and song titles. A dud left you with gambler's despair. The reward for striking gold, however, was a who-dared-won bliss, possibly unknowable in an age when music is cheaper than tap water.

One June day in 1987, I was in a record shop in Great Malvern, my hometown. I had flirted with buying the dusty cassette of Joni Mitchell's *Blue* for many months. The singer's name caught my eye, for obvious reasons. The cover was a classy white-on-blue photograph of the artist's face. It wasn't trying too hard to impress. I had sat my final A level the previous day and my school life was over, for ever. Until the exam results were published in August, my life was a blank Scrabble tile. I told Joni's white-on-blue face, *OK, today's the day I'm getting you out of here.* I paid, slotted the cassette into my knock-off Walkman and pressed play.

Good God. The next thirty-five minutes transformed my understanding of what songs could do and what singers could be. Firstly, Joni Mitchell's voice is a living thing of contradictions: it warbles with vibrato but is astringent and harsh, too; it's acrobatic yet grounded; vulnerable yet indestructible; mannered and octave-straddling, yet as natural as breathing or speech. Secondly, the instrumentation. The five-a-side of songs on *Blue* are stripped back to a guitar with atypical tunings; an Appalachian dulcimer drone (me neither); a lick of percussion or slide guitar; and a piano. That's your lot. The lack of clutter makes space for my 'thirdly': the album's consummate lyrics.

The opening track, 'All I Want', is a love song, but not like anything on *Top of the Pops* or my parents' Neil Diamond or Barbra Streisand records. The lines are made of everyday vocabulary assembled in rhymes – 'shampoo' and 'renew' – that I'd never encountered before. I realised how lazy most lyrics are, and absorbed the album's first lesson: when writing is good, people pay attention for fear of missing out on the next fresh pleasure.

'My Old Man' is built of Joni's swooping voice, one undulating piano and nuanced emotions. In 1987 I'd never been in love, much less fallen out of it, so I doubt I was conscious that the affair described in this song contains the seed of its own ending, or at least evolution, though perhaps I somehow intuited it. The ache in 'Little Green' was palpable without knowing that the girl in the song is the daughter that the teenage, penniless, unmarried Joni Mitchell had given up for adoption.

One consequence of musical purchases being so fraught with risk for my generation was that we remember the 'virgin plays' of albums for the rest of our lives. A midsummer mist had half-submerged the Malvern Hills. The sun was a pale disc, like a torch behind a sheet. Abbey Road, leaving Malvern to the south, was all bright murk. I passed stern Victorian houses, tall, pointed and subdivided into flats even then, and old trees with young person leaves. When I reached the end of Great Malvern and the beginning of Poolbrook Common, 'Carey' came on in its upbeat glory with congas and strumming. For a young person whose most exotic jaunt had been around the youth hostels of North Wales, the song's setting – a lamplit room, a Mediterranean breeze, a holiday fling – made me yearn to be somebody else, anywhere but here.

The last song on side A, 'Blue', is linked by colour to 'Little Green'. Who is 'Blue' sung to? Is Blue a person, another lover, the singer's own soul? The ennui of success and excess? Or simply the colour blue? Non-specificity and vagueness are not the same, and the former can magnetise and evoke. Like Mona Lisa's smile, the song doesn't answer the questions it asks. I remember stopping under a chestnut tree to shelter from a sudden shower, and the static hiss of the tape layering over the sound of the rain. This doesn't go with the sun-and-mist part of the memory, but that's memories for you.

Side B starts with 'California', a song infused with homesickness and a longing for acceptance. I crossed Peachfield Road on the southern edge of the common and set out on the track crossing the Worcestershire Golf Club's sloping course. The lyrics were flecked with humour. Could the dancing redneck she met on a Grecian isle be Carey? A character from side A cropping up on side B? My future writer self stored the idea on a shelf marked *Don't Forget*. 'California' yearns to set off; the next song, 'This Flight Tonight', is about the journey, and it isn't going well. The possible diptych gave me an early instance of what I grandly call the Propinquity Effect: when neighbouring units of art influence each other and create a third penumbral unit. Put a red lamp next to a blue lamp and you get a purple zone. Once you start looking for this in art, you'll find it everywhere.

My memory says I'm halfway across the golf course when I hear Joni's much-covered 'River' for the first time in my life. It's a watershed song on the album. Prior to this, love is present and, for the most part, celebrated; from hereon in, love is a source of pain. 'River' starts, jarringly, with a couple of bars evoking 'Jingle Bells' and a line about cutting down trees. What is sadder than losing love except losing love at Christmas? The self-scrutiny is stark. Here is an artist, unpeeled. How could Joni stand it? The song offers no solution, no way to make it right – only the unfulfillable wish for a frozen river to skate away on, into the winter's night.

'A Case of You' is a still darker song than 'River', about the scars of love. The title suggests a nasty infection as well as a box of vintage wine, and the song's boast – of being able to drink 'a case of you' and still be standing – is a hollow one. Love *is* intoxicating, and the craftiest part of the intoxication is to make you believe you're seeing things clearly when you aren't.

Blue closes with 'The Last Time I Saw Richard' – a title that could be a short story by Dorothy Parker or John Cheever. The song describes a dialogue between Joni and her ex, Richard, as if we are now twelve months after 'A Case of You'. The two have got over each other, it seems, but Richard has got over love itself. Joni is afraid of the belief that love is a thing one grows out of – that the cynicism of 'A Case of You' is the truth. The song is a masterpiece and, in its pairing of 'figure skater' and 'coffee percolator', has one of the seventies' best rhyming couplets. Richard's jadedness suggests a tawdry awakening from the idealism of sixties counterculture. The song ends with Joni going to her bar, sitting alone in a corner and drowning her disillusionment and the passing of Richard into a life more ordinary. These sad cafe days, she sings, are 'only a phase'. If you say so, Joni.

The songs on Blue are pages torn from a raw autobiography. I had never heard anything like it. (Kris Kristofferson's response to the album was reportedly, 'Joni! Keep something of yourself!') Yet you don't play Blue thinking, 'How weak': through the alchemy of art, vulnerability is turned to armour. The album was also my first encounter with truthful songs of female experience and agency. (Kate Bush's work was a sole exception.) Time and the changing world have not been kind to many albums that mattered to me as a kid, but Blue is art, evergreen and ageless.

My final paragraph will read like a novelist's embellishment, but it's not. In the last hundred yards of my walk from Great Malvern, I turned in to the estate where my parents lived and stepped off the pavement for a mother and her very young daughter. The girl piped up: 'Look, Mummy, that man has a wire coming out of his ear!' Her mother smiled my way and I realised that her daughter was talking about my Walkman – and me. Nobody had ever referred to me as a man before. I'm still working out what one is, half a lifetime later.

Sarah Hall

OK Computer by Radiohead (1997)

Music is a great recalling device. Some songs take you back to particular experiences, periods of life, or even a single seismic event. But I'm not very good at retreating into memories: relived narratives, grand romantic nostalgias, past times, they seem to collapse when I try. I prefer an optimistic, sensual now. Does that make me some kind of presentist? Maybe. One of the bands I like best has this exact effect – an amplification of the moment, so the feeling when listening is a kind of enhancement of life in real time, rather than past references.

I've been listening to Radiohead for more than twenty years. I picked up on them around the time of *The Bends* in 1995, when it seemed every amateur band was trying to do a cover of 'High and Dry'. While I was studying at St Andrews in Scotland I worked in a bar, the West Port

Hotel, then famous for unusual food (pickled octopus baguettes), high-grade coffee, art exhibitions, live music, free-pouring of spirits, local and international punters – lots of them on the creative writing and philosophy courses or at the Centre for the Study of Terrorism and Political Violence. Kate (KT) Tunstall and Kenny Anderson (King Creosote) both played at the West Port regularly in former incarnations, so I should say any cover versions were remarkably good. When *OK Computer* was released in 1997, I'd saved up enough money from the bar work to visit a friend from my writing course in New York. I was listening to 'Let Down' as the plane descended over Manhattan and I got my first, stupefied look at the city. I listened to 'No Surprises' while getting tattooed in Fun City Tattoo on St Mark's, by the extraordinary and terrifying artist Jonathan Shaw.

Perhaps such experiences would have been awesome anyway, but the album is so layered, imaginative, spatial and strange that, like the city, it is its own dreamworld. Like a great short-story collection, the songs have continuity but are atomised, experimental, synthetic and orchestral, soulful, frightening, intelligent, and deeply moving. The band is a brilliant combination of talented musicians, but Thom Yorke has a voice with timbre somewhere between the angel of death and a flaming, impervious martyr on a pyre. There's something very intimate and connecting about his vocals, so they seem to inhabit the mind. It's the combination of dynamic tone and the abstract, poetic, meaningful lyrics – a quality of inner narrative, the voice of your thoughts.

The album, the city, the experiences, all came together and would go on to help create one of my novels, *The Electric Michelangelo*. It should be an album of concrete, locational reference. But it isn't. Every time I listen to *OK Computer* it feels unburdened, freely transportive. I'm not reliving that time in my twenties or remembering skyscrapers at sunset, the frightening needle. Last time I listened to it I was driving through flat, dun-coloured Norfolk farmland, which became no less cinematic, no less exceptional or atmospheric than New York City under the effect of the music. I don't know how exactly, but the album always does what it did then: enhance current experiences, intoxicate anew.

Fiona Mozley

Cassadaga by Bright Eyes (2007)

I first heard *Cassadaga* while sitting on my ex-boyfriend's single bed. It was 2007, I was newly arrived at university, and I spent most of my time listening to music through his high-end loudspeakers, and hiding from the world. I had never been too keen on the 'singer-songwriter' trope – a label which, for me, evoked earnest crooners whisper-singing cod-poetry, their mouths held too close to the microphone. I thought Conor Oberst of Bright Eyes might be one of these, and initially gave the band a wide berth. Then I listened to *Cassadaga* properly.

The name comes from a town in Florida known for its mediums and dubbed the Psychic Capital of the World. It begins with a track called 'Clairaudients (Kill or Be Killed)', which presents a recording of one such soothsayer advising a restorative trip around America, overlaid on a sweeping orchestral arrangement that soon gives way to an acoustic guitar and Oberst's melancholic voice. Over the course of the album, Oberst makes predictions of his own. And he tells stories. There are glimpses of artists, session musicians, travellers, drifters, country singers, love affairs with older women, and the collapse of the World Trade Center: from the roof of a friend's place, he watches an empire end, as he sings in 'Cleanse Song'.

Oberst has been compared to Bob Dylan, a connection that must become tiresome and one I only mention out of a desire to assert their differences. It is true that both use voice and guitar to spit state-of-the-nation invectives. But while early Dylan captured the political energy of his generation, Oberst's songs are filled with ambiguities, missed opportunities and forlorn hope. He sings of whittled dreams, the wisdom of fools, seeds that never grow. *Cassadaga* takes 1960s idealism and twists it unexpectedly.

Maybe it's evasive to choose an album so defined by its lyrics. In so doing I'm giving myself an easier task. It is simpler to find the language to describe poetry than music: the operation of an unexpected time signature, a striking interval, a softly plucked string, the strange effect such things have on the human pulse. The band takes its cue from folk, Americana and country – a soundscape that, perhaps like any, is context-specific. The twang of a spruce-top guitar will always elicit images of the sweeping forests in which that spruce was felled; the fiddle (strangely distinct from the violin, though they are the same object) conjures campfires and ecstatic dancing. But, the music of *Cassadaga* goes beyond folksy nostalgia. Any acoustic tweeness is offset by distorted electronic interventions. The album's music (like its lyrics) holds up the sounds, voices, images and ideas of a bygone era, only to discard them irreverently.

It wasn't love at first listen, but a fascination that developed slowly, and one that has endured. I have listened to *Cassadaga* every couple of weeks for over a decade, and every time I do, I hear something new.

Esi Edugyan

Maxinquaye by Tricky (1995)

In 1995, as I was finishing my first year of university, I found myself lurking nervously outside the Commodore Ballroom in Vancouver, hoping to interview Tricky. I'd come with a boy I'd been dating for three years but whose fear of getting trapped on the West Coast meant the end was surely near. On that night we shuffled about in the cold of a dim May afternoon with a smatter of other student reporters, all of us anxious at the idea that Tricky might not turn up – or, more frighteningly, that he would.

Tricky's moodiness was legendary by then. The backstage fights with other musicians. The rocky love affair with Björk. The shouting matches with journalists who asked too eagerly about his childhood traumas. But I understood why they might ask – those traumas seemed to pervade the music. I have listened to *Maxinquaye* hundreds of times and each experience feels fresh and vibrant but laden too with the scars of the past. It is that rare album whose meaning seems to shift even as it provokes old griefs.

I still recall my first encounter with 'Ponderosa'. Martina Topley-Bird's scratchy, near-whispered vocals; the music itself, which sounds as if someone were gleefully playing a xylophone made of human ribcages – I was staggered. Never before had I heard such strange intensity. From the cover of Public Enemy's 'Black Steel in the Hour of Chaos', which in Tricky's iteration plays with notions of gender, to the dreamy sensuality of 'Pumpkin', *Maxinquaye* shocks and arrests. It is music to slap you out of complacency: unsettling, and filled at times with great ecstasy and creeping unease. The album expressed all the anxiety of the nineties but remains, in the end, larger than itself – a manic, genre-shattering, bombastic lament.

Tricky did eventually turn up that day. He arrived as from nowhere like a haunting, and he was everything we had not expected: small-statured, soft-spoken, unassuming. He answered every question put to him, no matter how silly or circuitous. I was too shy to speak, only scratched down his answers. But just when things were wrapping up, he leaned in and said, 'Does anyone have anything they didn't get to ask?'

I cleared my throat and, in a wisp of a voice, said, 'How are you dealing with fame?'

He fixed me with a considered look, and finally shrugged. 'I just don't care, that's all. I just don't care.'

And that seemed the essence of his aesthetic – this desire to turn from the light, to look away from the spectacle into the absorbing darkness.

He let us all into that evening's show for free, and it was a concert that has stayed with me throughout the years. I would eventually abandon journalism, and in the end my boyfriend would leave me for the East Coast, but the music remained.

David Hepworth

Sail Away by Randy Newman (1972)

I bought *Sail Away* on 1 July 1972 at a shop in Palmers Green, north London, called Opus Records. The night before, my girlfriend and I had been out seeing the J. Geils Band play a midnight show at the Lyceum off the Strand. Afterwards we dined on Wimpy and chips and then trudged to King's Cross to await the opening of the suburban line to take us to her home. I bought the record the following morning. We sat in bed listening to it and looking through the French windows into the garden.

Men, particularly young men, have to decide to like the musician before they allow themselves to like the music. I'd already decided I approved of Randy Newman. His songs had been hits for Alan Price and Dusty Springfield. However I wasn't entirely prepared for how dry he was when performing them himself as he did on *Sail Away*. If I was honest, I preferred the tracks like 'Last Night I Had a Dream' and 'You Can Leave Your Hat On'. These featured Ry Cooder and sounded more like the West Coast rock I favoured.

I watched Newman on *The Old Grey Whistle Test* when he visited. My enjoyment of 'Burn On' was increased by his saying it was written about 'the only river to be so polluted it was declared a fire risk'. He also played 'Political Science'. At the time, this seemed like a wildly exaggerated lampoon of American isolationism. Half a century later, its threat to 'drop the big one' on any nation that doesn't respect the Stars and Stripes could be a 140-character memo from Trump's White House.

Over the years, I've come to suspect it's the record's dryness that makes it endure. That and its ruthless lack of sentiment. You simply wouldn't be allowed to make it today. Randy Newman is the master of the unguarded thought. He had always given his best songs to his most reprehensible characters: the slaver in 'Sail Away', the Harvey Weinstein figure in 'You Can Leave Your Hat On', even the condescending deity in 'God's Song (That's Why I Love Mankind)' who only loves humans because they are just so needy. The interesting thing about unworthy thoughts is everybody has them.

The girlfriend and I are grandparents now. We push the babies in the park, secretly singing 'Memo to My Son' to ourselves, saving particular relish for the verse about how we can't wait for them to grow up and realise how smart their grandparents are. Randy Newman, of course, puts it a lot better than that.

Joe Dunthorne

Black Sunday by Cypress Hill (1993)

It's a Sunday afternoon in 1994 and I am twelve years old, sitting on the floor of my attic room, holding Scabeiathrax the Bloated to the light, admiring the septic wounds on his belly that it took me two days to paint. On the carpet, the rest of my Forces of Chaos are lined up for battle against my neighbour's Wood Elves. I watch him neaten his ranks of bureaucratic archers. If I want to defeat this hideous pragmatism, I will need to make use of my home advantage.

I go into my older sister's room and find a tape that – judging by the cover art – looks like it will perfectly soundtrack the victory of darkness. On the cover are the words *Black Sunday* written in gothic font, a parental advisory sticker, a hill built from skulls and graves, and the silhouette of a spooky tree. Perfect. Presumably heavy guitar music. I put it in the machine and press play. The first notes are a slowed-down horn, an eerie klaxon. I don't know it then but this is a warning knell. I am about to be conscripted into that most frightening army of all: middle-class white boys who love gangster rap.

From that day on, I listened to *Black Sunday* constantly. I learned the lyrics, usually interpreting them through the lens of my narrow life experience. When B-Real said, 'My oven is on high when I roast the quail', it seemed a moment of endearing domesticity. I would only learn later that quail, in this instance, was both a low-yield marijuana strain known for its smooth and creamy flavour, and a reference to the Republican vice president at the time the album came out, Dan Quayle.

Most of the lyrics are about smoking weed and most are not subtle. There are songs called 'I Wanna Get High', 'Hits From the Bong' and 'Legalize It'. I knew nothing about getting stoned. The great achievement of *Black Sunday* is that DJ Muggs's production allows even the straightest listener – the prepubescent boy playing Warhammer – to feel stoned, to feel, in fact, utterly baked, without ever having to inhale. When B-Real croons, 'I want to get high, so high', he is audaciously out-of-tune – like when you hear someone singing to themselves with their headphones on. His lack of self-consciousness can only be, we presume, blissfully narcotic. There's the stumbling double bass, scratchy drums and that spooky horn. The album veers between tales of cartoonish violence and stoner life, all narrated over funk and soul samples that have been elegantly deranged.

When I listen to this album today, I feel a little sorry for Cypress Hill. What can they rap about now that marijuana is legal in California? I also feel nostalgic for my twelve-year-old idea of how great getting stoned would be, before I discovered the paranoia and my underlying mental health issues. For this reason, listening to *Black Sunday* remains my favourite way to get blazed.

Suzanne Moore

Fresh by Sly and the Family Stone (1973)

I love *Fresh*. I love it for its cover: Sly Stone in the air, flying like a leather sex insect; black against white. The image, by Richard Avedon, is supernatural to me. This, and the cover of Lou Reed's *Transformer*, makes me tingle still. I had a boyfriend who painted them for me, which was the best art I had ever seen. Sort of.

This was the olden days and we had to make our own entertainment. The boyfriend was an attempt at that. I was fifteen and making the most crucial decisions of my life. What music to play. I liked some hippyish music – but then I heard the siren call. It was Sly Stone's voice. And I was gone. I played 'In Time', the first track, over and over again. It mesmerised me. The bassiness of it, the way it comes in and out. All present tense. Apparently Miles Davis did the same thing: he played it on repeat to his band for thirty minutes. So there is something a girl in Ipswich and Miles Davis had in common.

Miles, seventeen years older than Sly, recognised him as a peer. I love that – Miles being outfoxed by Sly. Who isn't? The thing here is that it's all drum and bass, stripped down but lifted high into the mix. It's a revolution. 'If You Want Me to Stay' is one of my all-time favourite tracks. Nile Rodgers once told me this was a coded message from Sly to his record company. There were difficulties, shall we say. I don't know, as I just hear a song about leaving, and I love songs about leaving as they make me feel powerful.

Who knows exactly what Sly *is* singing about half the time? Coke. Pep. Getting Down. Qué Será, Será. It's slightly out of it, but totally on it. Falling apart and then coming absolutely together. Something to do with rhythm itself. It's stupid to say I love funk as that's like saying I love breathing, but what I really like is this dark, intoxicated, yearning funk. It's all there in his growl of slink and joy, which is pure libido. You see it on the cover, you hear it on the record. The skin he is in.

Without Sly there would be no Prince, no Outkast, no Frank Ocean. He still looks and sounds to me like something future not past. But it's his voice. There is just nothing better in this world than Sly Stone's purr. If he doesn't make you feel real you must already be dead.

Ben Okri

Kind of Blue by Miles Davis (1959)

There are some rare albums that seem to lift from their physical condition and become part of the decor and mood of a life. They seem not to be music any more but one of the things that shape you, like the home you grew up in, or your earliest toys, the fragrance of your mother's hair, or the street where you first fell in love. Though music eminently has this capacity, it is often the case that even the greatest music draws attention to itself as music. Very rarely does it become an invisible fact of a life, woven into it like clouds in the sky, or trees along a road.

Miles Davis's *Kind of Blue* first made itself real in my life on a rainy morning in Lagos, in the seventies, when for the first time I was alone in the house. I was around seventeen and the emptiness of the house brought me to something resembling an existential decision. I had to decide what I wanted to do with my life. All that morning while it rained, I had been thinking. And while I had been thinking, *Kind of Blue* had been playing on the turntable. The music passed into thought, then into the sonic space in which my decision played out in ways unknown to me. That is to say, the music passed into the silence of the mind. My decision, which cannot be elaborated here, has led, through the turns and revelations of life, to where I am now, and where I will be tomorrow. That day there was Miles and Mozart and the rain and the smells and muted sounds of the ghetto where we had temporarily found ourselves, and my father's living room, with its invisible shrine; and throughout the room, throughout the house, there was the substantiality of his absence.

Kind of Blue has gone on playing a similar role in my life. Now it is so imprinted on my being that I don't need to listen to it to hear it. In some way it is always playing somewhere inside me, in a constant spirit loop, which is the result of such a saturation of listening. If such a thing as reincarnation exists, I would probably come back in a future life and, under past-life regression therapy, be convinced of the certainty that I had composed that music. But then I have always been an obsessive listener of music, and would inscribe a piece into my being if it spoke to me that deeply.

It is said, among the many strange things claimed for this album, that rather than being an urban paean, a dithyramb for the lost souls that need soothing, rather than being this tender lament, this heartfelt cool breeze on the hot skins of those who walked the narrow paths of the cities, it was really a Proustian moment of memory. Better to say it was a Milesian recollection of a moment when he was back in the South and heard music floating over the houses late in the night. That's the story at the plangent heart of the music.

But the music itself was made with Miles Davis's ensemble, consisting of a legendary group of musicians, including John Coltrane and 'Cannonball' Adderley on saxophone, Paul Chambers on bass, Jimmy Cobb on drums, Bill Evans – and on one track Wynton Kelly – on piano. The album was recorded in New York, at Columbia's 30th Street Studio, and every track is redolent of the mood of that city, alchemised to such a degree that it has in it the essence of cities and their solitudes, their wistful air of stoicism and coiled repose.

What was unique about the recording is that it brought out the best of the classical tradition and the improvisation at the heart of jazz itself. For many years Miles Davis had been chafing against the limitations of bebop, and even jazz as it was perceived at the time. It seems to be the case that innovators are often also heretics. They ask the fundamental questions that horrify the orthodoxies of their art. 'What is jazz?' Miles Davis used to ask, famously. Equally famous was his saying that he had white players in his band because he didn't want the music to sound too black. This from an artist who celebrated the power, and the agony, of being black.

The album, released in my birth year, was based on modality. It was created on little rehearsal and with the band having only the sketchiest notion of what they were to play. They had just hints of melodic lines on which to improvise. There were five tracks in all, recorded on two separate dates with about a month intervening. The result was what is considered one of the greatest albums ever recorded. Its influence transcends music.

It begins with what seems like low-key uncertainty and slides into a call and response that's like limpid poetry, wreathed with an impressionistic silvery melancholy and muted joy. Something indefinable haunts the music, some sorrow, some calm in the trumpet glissandos, something quiet that pierces the bones. It is that rare thing in all art: the perfect distillation of a spirit, a time and a genius.

I listened to it at the beginning of my writing life and it was one of the pieces of music I listened to all through writing *The Famished Road*. It helped keep me sane through the long, lonely nights and wild flights of imagination, always bringing me back home.

Now I listen to the silence while I write, because all the music I need is playing in me, in a spiritual, kind of blue way.

Olivia Laing

Automatic for the People by R.E.M. (1992)

Automatic for the People always seems to me like an autumn album, muted and piercing at the same time. It's music for listening to in the bath or maybe far out to sea. It was released just before I went to sixth-form college and is tied inextricably in my mind with the long walk from the bus stop in my dead-end Hampshire village, a straight road through a scattering of council houses to a new estate in what used to be farmland.

I'd fallen in love that summer and had my heart broken for the first time. Every afternoon, I'd walk home alone, past the tattered roses, and go up to my bedroom, papered with torn pictures of the Manic Street Preachers and *My Own Private Idaho*, any gaps covered in scribbled lines from Burroughs and Faulkner. I'd sprawl on the carpet with my typewriter, a pair of scissors and a pile of my sister's discarded copies of *i-D* and *The Face* and spend the long evenings making zines about late roses and November skies, the enormous feelings of being sixteen. The sadness of Michael Stipe's voice seeped under my skin, creating a convivial fug of melancholy.

I had a penfriend back then with beautiful spiky writing and she sent me a letter once with the lyrics of 'Find the River' twisted around the envelope. The litany of flower names – bergamot, bayberry, indigo – entangled itself with a book I was reading at the same time, *Modern Nature* by Derek Jarman. Both felt like artefacts from the Aids crisis. I don't think Stipe had yet come out, but his emaciated form on *Top of the Pops*, gaunt and ecstatic, dancing as if he was deep in a trance, fuelled rumours at school that he had Aids. He didn't, but the album was, he later said, riven by his own feelings of mourning and anxiety, porous and brimming with tenderness and vulnerability.

My favourite song was 'Nightswimming', its slow piano turning circles, Stipe's voice painfully clear and aching against lush little tendrils of orchestration. For years, I put it on every compilation tape I made, each with a painstakingly hand-collaged cover. It's up there with 'Duchess' by Scott Walker, 'Thoughts of You' by Dennis Wilson and 'Koochie Ryder' by Freaky Realistic in its capacity to conjure the specific gravity of that room, my first real studio, its air dense with a nineties funk of white musk and patchouli. Years later, I wanted to call my first book 'Find the River', in gratitude. What was it I wanted to say thank you for? The company, I suppose; the idea that difficult emotions might be companionable when shared, might even be the fuel for something gorgeous, something that sustains me still.

Neel Mukherjee

Mozart's *Piano Concertos in D minor and A major*
performed by Clara Haskil (1956)

'The past is not for living in,' wrote John Berger. It
is difficult to go back in time to an originary point,
unlearning everything that one has learnt since to
recover the pristineness and radical innocence of the first
moment. Wonder, unlike surprise, never fades; it just
gets buried deeper and deeper until excavation becomes
almost impossible. All that I have made my business
to know about Mozart in the forty-two years between
now and when I first heard, at the age of eight, his piano
concertos in D minor (KV 466) and A major (KV 488),
played by Clara Haskil in a 1956 recording issued by
Philips, intervenes peskily in that attempt at recovery.

Did I know that 'Klavierkonzert' meant piano concerto
at that age? Did I know what a concerto was? It goes without

saying that concepts such as d-moll and A-dur came later and had to be learned; also the Köchelverzeichnis catalogue numbers, what a cadenza is, what allegro assai and romanze signified. But did I work out then that *Clara Haskil: Klavier* meant *name of pianist: instrument*? Yet I remember perfectly – or think I can remember perfectly, for what is memory but fiction? – other things. The huge black pen-and-ink drawing of a chandelier on the album cover. The fat red band on top with 'Mozart' in large white letters. The incomprehensible German words (it was a German LP). The Philips logo, followed by 'Minigroove 33⅓'. The smell – incense, Sunday chicken curry, naphthalene – in the piano teacher's room in Ballygunge, Calcutta. The stand of severely pollarded, variegated croton trees outside that I could see from the woven cane chair on which I was sitting.

But all these were secondary to the music that was pouring out, like a new, unnamed kind of river, from the turntable into my ears. These were new sounds; they constituted what I can only call a plenitude. To write about it is always already late. How easily dread transformed to melody then kept effortlessly commuting between the two, before the piano stepped in, in the first movement of the D minor concerto. I remember my confusion: which should I listen to, the orchestra or the piano? How were they talking together and taking turns? Because it *was* a conversation, and even my eight-year-old self knew it then. At times, Haskil gave the impression that she was playing with six hands – how could so many notes be under the command of only ten fingers? – and at other times, she was letting only the lightest of her thoughts barely brush the keys.

Pages turning, musicians clearing their throats, adjusting their seats: how alive and affecting, how real these traces of the *making* of music were. To this day I find perfect, cleaned-up sound in a recording not much different in effect from the industrial antiseptic odour of hospital interiors. That hint of hiss in the hinge between the solo piano's lead and the orchestra's following in the mighty adagio of the A major concerto – life resides for me there.

Neil Gaiman

Diamond Dogs by David Bowie (1974)

Diamond Dogs is my favourite David Bowie album, which means it's more or less (take a little Lou Reed, give a little Elvis Costello) my favourite album.

Which is odd, because it's not the best David Bowie album. It's definitely not the most iconic. It didn't change anything for ever in the way that other Bowie albums changed the face of music. It exists at the cigarette-stub-end of Bowie's Ziggy haircut, as a resting place for songs from a dead musical based on *1984*, and a pencil sketch of an ambitious science-fiction project that never happened.

I had discovered Bowie in 1972. I was just twelve years old, a scholarship boy in a minor prep school in Sussex, obsessed by science fiction and fantasy and horror, with no music that spoke to me directly. And then I heard the song 'Space Oddity' on the radio, and I got the same buzz from Bowie that I did from science fiction. A friend had *Hunky Dory*, and I listened to it. My cousin Adam had *The Rise and Fall of Ziggy Stardust and the Spiders from Mars*.

I was already a thirteen-year-old fan when *Diamond Dogs* came out. I would sit and draw Bowie's face with the *Aladdin Sane* lightning bolt. I put the *Diamond Dogs* cover poster up on the inside of my bedroom door. I could watch the half-dog Bowie freak from my bed. It was the version that had been in the centre pages of *Sounds* before the album was released, and it was the uncensored, original Guy Peellaert image: the word above the dog-man's head was ALIVE, not BOWIE, and the dog was unquestionably male.

Diamond Dogs is not a coherent story, but I'm not sure I wanted a coherent story. The inner sleeve's photographs of a broken city, as if seen in a damaged kaleidoscope, aren't coherent either, but they paint a place. And the world of *Diamond Dogs* is a place.

My love of *Diamond Dogs* is not about the songs, or the story, or even the fragments of science fiction that glisten through the album. Orwell's *1984* is there, obviously, but it seemed littered with so much more than that: mutant eyes and crying lizards, all in a rotting city that had once been New York. (Samuel R. Delany's novel *Dhalgren* would not be published until a year after *Diamond Dogs* was released, but they could have escaped from the same ecstatically decaying city.) It's not even the juxtaposition of delicious images, produced (I learned a year later from the BBC *Cracked Actor* documentary) by Burroughsian cut-ups and randomness.

No, it's my favourite album because it was *mine* – in a way no other Bowie album had been, or would be again. I had spent a year or more listening to the albums recorded in the distant past, when I was young: everything from the Deram *David Bowie* album to *Ziggy Stardust*. I loved them all, but they had existed before I found them.

Diamond Dogs came out in January 1974. It was the best album because of ear candy like 'Rebel Rebel'; because it contained complex lyrics on 'Sweet Thing' and 'Candidate' that made me feel like I was being shown a twelve-hour drama through a letterbox slot; because the opening monologue pronounces the album unashamed science fiction; because it sent me to the school library aged thirteen to borrow *1984*, back then only a decade away; because the track listing on the cassette was all jumbled for reasons of time, so that story, whatever it was, and that sequence was what I first encountered and responded to, built up in my head, which meant that it would be another thirty-two years until I realised I could reorder the track listing on my computer and listen to *Diamond Dogs* in a way that felt right to me.

It's not that *Diamond Dogs* made me a science-fiction writer. (I didn't really grow up to be a science-fiction writer.) But it fed the part of me that made things up, that fell for dystopias and mutants, for rotting skyscrapers and rats the size of cats, shaped the inside of my thirteen-year-old head and made me who I am.

So it's my favourite.

Tracey Thorn

Innervisions by Stevie Wonder (1973)

My brother bought *Innervisions* when it came out in 1973. He would have been about nineteen, and I was ten, and not long afterwards he moved out, leaving a few of his records behind. Among them was this one, which for some reason was sort of adopted by my dad, by temperament and generation more of a Frank Sinatra/ George Shearing sort of man. He took a shine to Stevie Wonder and for a while when he put on a record at Sunday lunchtime, instead of it being Nat King Cole, or Eydie Gormé, it would be *Innervisions*. My sister and I both loved it too, and so the record represented a rare moment when we were all in musical agreement.

And what a giant of an album it is. *Innervisions* is musically diverse and varied and Stevie plays almost every instrument on it, in that crazy-talented way that prefigured Prince. It's a lyrically profound, conscious record; visionary and impassioned, full of images of struggle and transcendence yet packed with tunes and hits: 'Golden Lady', 'All in Love Is Fair', 'Don't You Worry 'bout a Thing', 'He's Misstra Know-It-All'. And perhaps its greatest track, 'Living for the City', a stirring, anti-racist groove anthem.

I remember being overwhelmed by that breathless spoken-word section in the middle, the song suddenly becoming a movie as the music breaks down and is replaced by the sound of traffic and the voice of a young man arriving on a Greyhound bus: 'New York', he exclaims, 'just like I pictured it, skyscrapers and everything!' Trouble arrives, and chaos ensues, and before you know it he has been crushed by racist cops and prison guards, and then back comes the song – Stevie's furious, clinging-to-hope final verses, his voice gritty with near despair. Pop songs could be so ambitious in those days – musically accomplished, full of serious intent and lyrical dexterity, *and* danceable. I don't know what else you'd ever need.

So this is an album which I admire unreservedly, and for which I also have strong sentimental feelings. It reminds me of home, and of my whole family, at a moment when we were all in unexpected accord and hit a kind of communal musical high-point that we never bettered.

Musa Okwonga

Aquemini by Outkast (1998)

As a musician myself, my most important album keeps changing – once it was *The Score* by the Fugees, at another time *Crooks & Lovers* by Mount Kimbie. But *Aquemini* came into my life just before I started university and hasn't left since. With the exception of the Wu-Tang Clan, I had never seen black men so creative, so fearless. This album has everything: breadth, depth, length, supreme storytelling, wild, almost reckless divergence of moods; at turns triumphant and melancholic, but always mesmerising. It's an otherworldly piece of music, the kind of thing you could play to aliens as proof of how sublime humans can be. I love *Aquemini* as much as I love the collected short stories of Kurt Vonnegut – every time I return to both works, I find some new way of looking at the human condition.

I also love *Aquemini* because it shows, in the most thrilling fashion, what happens when two songwriters utterly trust each other. This is the album where Big Boi and André 3000 worked perfectly in tandem, and became far greater as a result. I listen to 'Chonkyfire' and think that Outkast, if they wished, could have made the greatest rap-rock album of all time. 'SpottieOttieDopaliscious' is still a gold standard for any poet who seeks to put their words to music. The title track is as wistful yet stirring as anything that hip hop has produced, and 'Rosa Parks' will fill dance floors for years to come.

I am obsessed with pieces of art that are wholly, superbly realised, because they are immediately timeless. They leave me with a sense of sadness whenever they draw to a close, the same way I feel when finishing a home-made meal with loved ones. *Aquemini* is a work that surges and lulls, that sprawls but never meanders; it's vast, contemplative, universal. Most of all, it's brave. They could have stuck to the formula, but they embraced autotune, funk, folk and more. André sang, Big Boi wrote hooks galore, they got George Clinton in the studio and went to work. The outcome was glorious.

Whenever unsure about the musical path I should take, I ask myself: 'What would Outkast do?' And the answer is always the same – risk everything, including ridicule and failure. Venture beyond the boundaries of all you've produced to this point. Try to make the kind of music that, decades from now, someone will idly slip on shuffle as their spacecraft moves from one galaxy to another; and, upon hearing it, they'll think: 'You know what, that's not half bad.'

Mark Ellen

The B-52's by the B-52's (1979)

I've just lowered the needle on this much-adored, crackling slab of vinyl to be ferried back to the outer reaches of science fiction. A bleeping digital pulse, a rackety backbeat and a shrill wave of synthesiser eventually usher in the camp, nasal tones of someone celebrating a planet where the air is pink, the trees are red and one of its deathless natives has escaped to Earth where she now drives a Plymouth Satellite.

Some albums hold a mirror to the soul, others offer wisdom that slowly registers through the passing years, but for me this eternally cheering companion simply strikes its dependable notes of comfort and nostalgia, as fresh and energetic as when it first touched down in 1979 – a crisp cartoon of sound and vision. Its cinematic lyrics and twanging surf guitar conjure images of a fading

America, of sixties dance moves and coast-bound classic cars in that delightfully upbeat age when people expected space travel in their own lifetime and nothing seemed impossible or remotely serious.

The five members of this magnificent band tooled up for their stage shows by raiding the yard sales of their local Athens, Georgia, the boys appearing in eye-watering Hawaiian shirts, the girls in garish stretch-fabric and towering bouffant wigs. Their songs were equally over-cranked and agreeable – love, for example, is represented as a red-hot volcanic eruption.

You weren't invited to make a personal connection with any of it, just to be richly entertained, to be transported to a sun-lit universe where poolside parties are in permanent swing, people have names like Crystal and Mercedes (as in the song '52 Girls'), and carefree types in vibrant leisurewear cavort as if in a beach movie, or lie sizzling after thick applications of 'tanning butter' (as in the glorious 'Rock Lobster', the track that inspired John Lennon to get back to the studio).

I still find this first album by the B-52's a charming slice of theatre, the irresistible soundtrack to an imagined world whose allure never fades. Some favourite records can be purely escapist. This flicks that switch every time.

Linda Grant

Hejira by Joni Mitchell (1976)

I first heard the title track of *Hejira*, with its images of vehicles, cafes and love's wars, in the autumn of 1976 in an apartment in a university town in Ontario. The previous year I had hitchhiked from Maryland to California, up to Washington State, diverting to Winnipeg to see a former boyfriend; then, leaving my man at a North Dakota junction, hitched to Minneapolis–Saint Paul and took a train back to New York. This life, on the road – a loose pearl on a taut thread; the sense of the vastness of the continent and love pulling you one way, freedom the other – was the preparation for hearing the album. I never heard in anyone but Joni Mitchell an account of what it was to want the refuge of the roads, as well as 'love that sticks around'. It was the great paradox of seventies feminism.

The album opens with a one-night stand with a rancher (reputedly Sam Shepard), moves on to a solitary drive across the desert remembering the aviator Amelia Earhart in the lonely clouds, then an affair with a younger man, before arriving at the title track. It is an album about longing, possessiveness and authenticity, and it stamped itself irrevocably on my life. It is the most personal album I own, personal about Joni Mitchell and personal about me. I never saw her perform live. I don't want to. I've no interest in sharing her with total strangers because none of this is about her, it's about me.

Hejira is the culmination of a series of five albums that starts with *Blue*, released in 1971. By the time it came out she had mastered the arts of poetry, storytelling and philosophy. Of course, none of this is cool or cynical or indifferent, and inevitably she was about to be savaged by a misogynist music industry and dismissed as a folkie by punk. Yet when I wrote about her a few years ago, I was astonished by the intensity of her male fan base. It turned out that she wasn't just speaking to young women but to the heart that loves and suffers. She is as great as Bob Dylan and Leonard Cohen. Greater.

Jason Cowley

The Colour of Spring by Talk Talk (1986)

I was not keen to tell friends that I'd been listening to Talk Talk. This was back in 1986. I'd always dismissed the band as synth-pop lightweights until one Friday evening I saw them on Channel 4's live music show *The Tube*. The two songs they showcased from their recently released third album, *The Colour of Spring* – 'Living in Another World' and 'Give It Up' – were complex and richly textured, and they were performed with an enthralling intensity. The band's singer-songwriter Mark Hollis, always a reluctant frontman, seemed enraptured but also somehow sad. He did not look at the camera. He was wearing small, round, John Lennon-style sunglasses and a wedding ring, his shirt was untucked and his longish hair was pulled into an unconvincing ponytail. He sang of being lost in a maze and of being unable to help himself find a way out of it.

Most notable was that Hollis and the band seemed utterly sincere. They meant it. How to account for the transformation in their music and manner?

Back then I was working as a clerk at the Electricity Council in London having failed to complete my A levels. It was a strange, melancholy period in my life. Each morning, I commuted on a coach from a small town on the Essex–Hertfordshire borders, where I lived with my parents, to Millbank, where our offices were located. It was a long, tedious journey – sometimes it took more than two hours and then I had to do it again in reverse in the evening – and I passed the time reading and listening to music on my Walkman.

What I still like so much about *The Colour of Spring*, all these years later, is that it captures a band in transition, leaving behind the old ways as they experiment with new forms and new approaches to making music. On a track such as 'April 5th' one can hear the celebrated sound of late Talk Talk struggling to emerge: Hollis's voice is hesitant, murmured, and the song's arrangement is minimal and spare as it fades inexorably into silence.

Mark Hollis withdrew from public life in the late nineties after the release of his first and last solo album, and he died after a short, unexplained illness in February 2019. He came to despise the music business but must have known he was revered as an uncompromising, visionary innovator; Talk Talk's final two albums,

Spirit of Eden and *Laughing Stock*, are considered 'post-rock' masterpieces.

I admire those albums, especially *Spirit of Eden* and its haunting, prayer-like closing piece 'Wealth', to which I have been listening repeatedly since Hollis died. But for me it all began with *The Colour of Spring*, and nowadays whenever I hear 'Living in Another World', I feel as if I am back on that commuter coach, it is dark outside (it is always dark), I am feeling confused, and Hollis's anguished vocals speak directly to and for me: help me find a way out of this maze.

Will Self

Astral Weeks by Van Morrison (1968)

I wouldn't exactly say it was my favourite album, but *Astral Weeks* is probably the album – considered as an album – that I've listened to most in my life. It is – almost all would acknowledge – a great album, and moreover one that's constituted by a suite of eight songs, one flowing seamlessly into the next, so as to give the whole the feel of a single through-composed piece. In fact, I don't think I've ever thought much about the individual tracks – for me, the quiddity of *Astral Weeks* is . . . the astral weeks I spent lying by the turntable, picking the needle up when it swirled across the inside of the disc, flipping that disc, then collapsing back on to the carpet as the achingly familiar chords of either the title track, or those of 'The Way Young Lovers Do', the first track on the second side, swelled in my hurting heart.

It was 1986, I was living in a cavernous flat off the Cromwell Road in west London lent to me by a wealthy friend. My only employment was doing a weekly cartoon strip for the *New Statesman* – and like its protagonist, Slump, I spent most of my time in bed. I'd like to claim I was a victim of the Thatcherite 'readjustment' – but mostly I was the victim of a ravening drug habit. Heroin, of course – it was the temper of the times – but also a lot of cocaine, injected, which scared the bejesus out of me. (As Ivan Morrison probably wouldn't say.) Sometimes I'd walk around the apartment with a needle stuck in my arm, the barrel of the syringe full of blood, and as I rhythmically pumped it, 'flushing' the solution of cocaine into my system, my heartbeats hammered in my ears as Van the Man strummed my heartstrings.

With the touching faith of the bourgeoisie in all professionals, I asked my GP for help – and he sent me to a psychiatrist who diagnosed me as a borderline schizophrenic and put me on a drug called Parstelin, a mix of so-called antidepressants and antipsychotics that was so strong I felt as if I were walking around buried up to my waist in mud with my brain full of sand. Which I didn't altogether mind, since it stopped me physically leaving the flat to score more coke. Instead I lay by the record player. I must've listened to *Astral Weeks* hundreds – if not thousands – of times. I was in love as well (pretty obviously), with an unattainable girl who lived in Notting Hill. So every time Van warbled about seeing the object of his desire strolling along Ladbroke Grove, I felt his words – as his great rival would put it – like a corkscrew to my heart.

I know every word, strum and nylon-string-squeak of *Astral Weeks* by heart. In the intervening thirty years, I've had several more periods of listening intensively to this album – I've read all about its recording; hell, I've even visited Cyprus Avenue, the unprepossessing suburban Belfast street that provides the mythopoeic landscape for the song of the same name. Yet I'm by no means a slavish Van Morrison fan; it's just that weird sedated period, of being at once death-borne and transcendent, venturing in the slipstream – between the viaducts of his dreams, and my own – that's left this album with me. For ever.

Sabrina Mahfouz

A Little Deeper by Ms. Dynamite (2002)

Skanking out to the golden-era garage beats in Ayia Napa nightclubs makes up many of my favourite memories. Darkness and AC-chilled air inside keeping us awake (shout out sambuca shots too) even as the sun and Levantine heat rose outside. Every summer from 2000 to 2006 our group of garage girls travelled from London, Wales, Bedford and Birmingham to the island of Cyprus to reunite and rave our way through a couple of months of dubious moneymaking, moped racing and daytime sleeping. We would hear the new UK sounds emerge right in front of us, as the boys we knew from all the incompatible postcodes played gigs at venues together in a way that would've been too hectic for musical evolution back home. And we were so used to a stage full of men that when Ms. Dynamite would occasionally come on – calling out the MCs for their objectifying, often derogatory yet normalised words about women, and giving a feminist speech at a 5 a.m. rave in the days before feminism was a word we even knew – we'd smile, gun-finger and clap for her, but we did not fully appreciate what we had.

Ms. Dynamite had the flow, vibe and lyrics to shut down any stage at any rave, and when her debut album *A Little Deeper* was released in 2002, she allowed us all to do exactly that. To go a little deeper into who we could be, who we wanted to be. To recognise the injustices all around us, not just in faraway places but those that were happening to us, even those that might be caused by us. To be heartbroken more articulately. To believe we could succeed in spaces dominated by the men that so many other female musicians told us implicitly or directly to seduce with our looks, our moves, our unconditional love.

The album gave us the singalong, head-nodding anthem 'Dy-Na-Mi-Tee', as well as the moving 'Brother', which dealt openly with depression, suicide, the pressures of family dynamics and the power of sibling solidarity. In British music, Ms. Dynamite is an under-celebrated icon. She brought us feminist, fun, socially conscious, garage-and-grime-infused music, long before it became packaged for mainstream success.

John Burnside

A Natural Disaster by Anathema (2003)

Back in 2003, a friend gives me a CD and says try this later when you have a quiet moment; and because I trust his taste, I do. It is by a band called Anathema and this, apparently, is their seventh album, but it comes as no surprise that I don't know them, because I've been wrapped up in one of my austere, nothing-after-1971 spells for a long time – one where I secretly know the history of rock music ended with Roy Harper's *Stormcock*.

Like all nerds, I start by listening for influences but it's immediately clear that *A Natural Disaster* is its own creature, a work of taut beauty and control. (Listening to this band many times since, I'm constantly reminded of the fact that a live tradition is not made by those who go before, but by those who, learning wisely from their best forerunners, shape and mould a communal body of work that will continue, constantly mutating, perennially ripe and fruitful.) What hit me so hard on that first play was the title track. It opens into a quiet, simple lyric, lines that glide into an agonised yet still restrained cry of recognition, not just of a pain that will never quite go away but (much, much worse) that this pain has its origins not in fate or bad luck but in some terrible yet probably quite everyday mistake the singer has made. An event now locked in an unchangeable past, it gives rise to the one note of unbearable urgency in the devastating chorus – 'No matter what I say/ No matter what I do/ I can't change what happened' – that runs on and on until some kind of acceptance kicks in.

Why this song should have hit me so hard (so hard, I admit, that I crumpled to the ground and sat, awed by the retelling of a story of my own, one I had kept buried for decades); why this song should have changed the course along which I had been blindly stumbling is personal, which is to say, of no great matter. What does matter, however, is the recognition of time's forward momentum, the understanding that when you have made the mistake of a lifetime, your one duty is to find not just a way to live with the consequences, but also some sustenance in its aftermath. As the poet Stephen Crane wrote, 'It is bitter – bitter . . . But I like it/ Because it is bitter/ And because it is my heart.'

Lionel Shriver

Last Exit to Brooklyn by Mark Knopfler (1989)

Alas, I've only seen the haunting film of *Last Exit to Brooklyn* once (correctly infer: it's not on Netflix), but I must have listened to Mark Knopfler's soundtrack hundreds of times. As most soundtracks do when viscerally married to the content they accompany, this one never fails to evoke the film in my mind: the grim warehouses, broken-down cars and vacant lots of a 1950s Brooklyn that the current residents buying nori snacks at Trader Joe's would never recognise; the unbearable sorrow of nearly every character; the horrifying gang rape of Tralala, the prostitute played by Jennifer Jason Leigh – an assault that, in an act of nauseous self-loathing, she deliberately invites.

Heavy on strings yet never schlocky, the hummable central theme captures a longing, sweetness and desire rapidly undermined by a sleazy off-key brass line and an ominous vibraphone. The feelings with which the opening track fills me are complex and contradictory: an aching sense of beauty, fullness and yearning, stunted by a sense of doom. This is a movie about characters who, despite their fundamental decency, will inflict the greatest injury on the people they love. Who will never rise above their circumstances. Whose best instincts are menaced not only by the malign forces you can hear pounding on kettledrums in the second track, but by their own self-hatred.

I'm not at all convinced that you need to have seen the film in order to enjoy the soundtrack, however. The heartbreaking sweetness of the more lyrical passages wrestling with and often arising from the turmoil of the darker tracks would surely affect any listener without reference to the story. I have to confess that this album often moves me to tears (come to think of it, this album always moves me to tears). Knopfler hits eternal notes of lost innocence, mourning and mortality – of tragic waste and dreams that will never materialise. Likewise, in the track titled 'Tralala', he calls up sassiness, sexiness and a sauntering sway down the way. You can see a pair of hips sashaying along the street, whether or not you specifically envision Jennifer Jason Leigh.

Another of my favourite soundtracks, to *Cal*, is also by Mark Knopfler. Unusually talented at expressing a movie's emotional progression, he is a dab hand, too, at ending up with a sequence of tracks that stands alone. Were I ever in a position to pick the composer for a film made from one of my novels, Knopfler would be top of the list.

Daljit Nagra

Meat Is Murder by the Smiths (1985)

Boys in thick leather jackets at our shop in Sheffield would have Queen, U2 and other names of solid rock bands daubed on the back with Tipp-Ex. A new name had started to appear on the jackets of these late teens, that of the Smiths. These boys were my age and they were inadvertently introducing me to a band I would come to grudgingly like. Grudgingly because these same jacketed boys would smash our shop windows and paint the shutters with racist slurs. Of a Friday or Saturday evening outside our shop, while sozzled on Thunderbird, they'd chant offensive songs.

By the mid-eighties, I'd heard enough of the Smiths on John Peel's radio show to know they were not a natural fit for the boys at our shop. The band won me over with their northern mischief, with their music-hall singer, Morrissey, who adorned his back pocket with daffodils and affected an earpiece. The first Smiths album I bought, which remains my favourite, is *Meat Is Murder*. As a vegetarian, I was drawn to its title track. In the age of Wham! and Duran Duran, the Smiths were post-meat, post-race, post-gender and treated death as a plaything. They sang of death in my favourite and most floppy-limbed song, 'Well I Wonder', with its Keatsian desperado who gasps for even a look of the beloved – oh! the poetry of Romanticism, of Goethe's yellow-shirted hero Werther. Death had never been so camp. In other songs, a girl at a fairground questions the length of the drop from a parachute, a boy enjoys swallowing nails, the speaker lies in bed weighing up life and death. I related to this album and its cassette comforts when I ran away from Sheffield to end up near Rusholme in Manchester, hoping to spot Morrissey and the Smiths guitarist Johnny Marr in Holland & Barrett by the tofu burgers.

Roland Barthes considers 'the grain of the voice', which he describes as the body in the voice. To me, Morrissey's voice had a grain of pure Englishness. It's a voice that locates itself as part of the north in social and political decline. It's a voice that soars over Marr's arpeggios and roots me in this nation of bittersweet memories. It's a voice of quaint English churchyards inside Victorian railings under rain; it's the sound of an English beach crying for custom; it smells of Arthur Askey and Kenneth Williams, of the backstage dressing room when the comedy's worn off; and when Morrissey yodels I taste bonfire parkin. I saw myself as an outsider listening in to the grain of that voice.

When seeking the charm of an English mood, I read Larkin or listened to the Smiths. Of death, Morrissey is our great rock star in the way Larkin is our great poet. But those who write about mortality only endure if they mock death, not if they become a mockery. Like Larkin, I'd have Morrissey leave the limelight, so I can love the best work before he smashes the shopfront of his own great tenderness.

Rachel Kushner

Mother Juno by the Gun Club (1987)

The richest stream of American punk rock is actually Mexican–American punk rock. It can be traced directly back to two self-taught wunderkinder whose lives collided: Jeffrey Lee Pierce, a second-generation Mexican (on his mother's side) from El Monte in East LA, and Kid Congo Powers, with two Mexican parents, from seven miles east in La Puente.

Their separate paths were parallel. As a teenager, Jeffrey Lee was the president of the Blondie fan club. Kid Congo Powers was the president of the Ramones fan club. They'd each gone alone to New York riding Greyhound, to check out the No Wave scene. Back at home in LA, Jeffrey Lee wrote for the music magazine *Slash*. Kid wrote the newsletter for the legendary LA band the Screamers. These two kindred boys met outside a Hollywood punk club one night in 1979. Kid was attracted to Jeffrey Lee's look: white vinyl trench coat, white cowboy boots. They bonded over a shared hunger for wild notes of influence not to be found locally. Jeffrey Lee told Kid he was starting a band, and that Kid could be the singer. 'I can't sing,' Kid said. 'Then you'll play guitar,' Jeffrey Lee said. 'I don't play guitar,' Kid responded, apologetically. 'I'll teach you,' said Jeffrey Lee. He gave Kid a Bo Diddley record and a slide guitar, tuned to an open E, along with a cassette of mood music: Delta blues, gunfighter ballads, Ornette Coleman, and what Jeffrey Lee summarised as 'lowlife Amerika'.

They formed a band. Jeffrey Lee sang. He was a savant vocalist with a spine-tingling caterwaul. He looked, as he sang on 'For the Love of Ivy', like an Elvis from hell. Kid Congo, on slide guitar, wore a gold blazer from Lansky Brothers in Memphis, where Elvis himself had shopped.

I was twelve when the Gun Club's first record, *Fire of Love*, was released, in 1981. I had an older brother and lived in a city (San Francisco) with a punk scene. I knew this music was cool, and this singer too, whose vibe was Robert Mitchum in *The Night of the Hunter*: an evil preacher in black leather, but with hair bleached to look like Deborah Harry's.

The first four Gun Club records still remind me of adolescence, of the desire to break something and/or be destroyed, a destruction that for a young person transmits as hope, because it is *energy*. Of all the Gun Club's records, *Mother Juno*, released in 1987, when I was

182

eighteen, shocks me most, with its beauty and depth. I listen to it still. It's lush and dreamy, and it's also hard. It's rock and roll. I remember the day I bought it. I was in college and went to Rasputin Records on Telegraph Avenue in Berkeley, brought it back to my apartment and played it over and over, mostly the second side (this was the era of vinyl). Even the wine-fuchsia hue of the album sleeve envelops me in feeling from that time. Not the context of the time (confusion, as a person with no idea why she was in college), but a feeling of wild possibility in the music itself, which obliterated context.

The unique sound of *Mother Juno* among Gun Club records is partly to do with the fact that Robin Guthrie, of the Cocteau Twins, produced it. It was recorded at Hansa Studios in Berlin. 'We blew people's minds,' Kid Congo later said about that record. They wanted a sound that linked back to their origins. East LA. Fierce music you'd hear from garages, while people worked on cars. By coincidence or not, Jeffrey Lee had stopped bleaching his hair at that point. For the first time in his life as a musician, he looked Latino. Perhaps the secret power of *Mother Juno* is intertwined with a determination to transcend stereotyped ideas about who owns what culture, what music.

The 'hit' from the album, 'The Breaking Hands', has a jangly, life-and-death shimmer that floats around the edges of Kid Congo's slide guitar like a moving gallery of luminous colours reflected from a mirrored ball.

Jeffrey Lee's voice is a yearning vibrato in a stripped-down atmosphere. The album has a grand and echoing but raw, bare sound. Hansa Studios is an old ballroom. After I saw photographs of it – a cavernous room with an ornate ceiling, parquet floors and huge chandeliers – I heard that room in the album.

I realise, writing this, that I've been listening to the song 'The Breaking Hands' for thirty-three years and it never bores me. It never gets old.

I love the whole record, but my two other obsessively repeated numbers are 'Yellow Eyes', which features guitar playing by Nick Cave and the Bad Seeds' Blixa Bargeld, and 'Port of Souls'. I don't know what to say about 'Port of Souls' except it holds in it some secret that I've convinced myself has to do with me: a secret I possess, about me, and that is eternally kept from me. I listened to it repeatedly when I was writing my last novel, *The Mars Room*. I even thought about titling the novel 'Port of Souls'. But the words alone are not enough. It is the music, the layered guitars and cool and mysterious feedback and Jeffrey Lee's voice, that transports. When I listen to the song now, I remember what I felt the first time I heard it. Which is to say, I remember what it felt like to want to exist only and totally in the present tense.

Jeffrey Lee Pierce died from drugs and alcohol in 1996, aged thirty-seven. For a while I held on to this dumb idea that he died on the 4th of July, as if to cure my disdain for patriotism. But it isn't true. Recently, I was talking to an old boyfriend about Jeffrey Lee, of having seen him play live in 1993, and how sad he seemed, how unhealthy he looked, in a too-small blazer, a Mao cap pulled down above his swollen face. This old boyfriend said, 'Gosh, I didn't even remember you were a Gun Club fan.' He's excused, though. A few years ago, he had a serious motorcycle accident that affected his memory. Otherwise, he never would have forgotten.

Ian Rankin

Solid Air by John Martyn (1973)

My favourite album is not set in stone: it changes every week or maybe every month. Having said that, give me an album at a certain age and it is mine for life, as Miss Jean Brodie might have said. So I'll settle for *Solid Air*.

I was not a shoo-in as a John Martyn fan. I was seventeen and liked Status Quo and Alex Harvey. When punk came along I would embrace it. A school pal called John Scott played me *Solid Air*, and I wasn't hooked. I could hear jazz and folk and soul. Anathema to me at the time. But John knew his music so this had to be good, didn't it? I duly bought the vinyl and started listening. My mum almost liked it – another mark against it – but I kept listening. It grew on me. And kept growing.

What's so special about *Solid Air*? Great musicianship, Martyn's voice – that of a whisky-soaked angel – and songs that defy categorisation. There are simple-sounding toe-tappers, extended improvisations, meditations on love, sin and death. The title track is Martyn's commemoration of his friend Nick Drake, while 'May You Never' is the song most people know. And then there's the raucous updated blues of 'I'd Rather Be the Devil' – a title so good I later borrowed it for a novel.

Punk came and went but *Solid Air* was still there. I became a student, then a PhD student, then a husband. Kids arrived. I moved houses and countries. Each time, when we moved, the first album on the turntable was *Solid Air*. It separates good sound systems from bad. And suddenly I'm a successful novelist and I've been invited onto *Desert Island Discs* (one of the last recordings Sue Lawley did). So I'm in London. The one song I can't live without is 'Solid Air'. I'm going to say that on air. Beforehand, I'm having lunch with my agent. And Martyn is with some mates at a nearby bottle-strewn table. And I can't go and talk to him. My one and only chance and I blow it. Oh well. The song and the album remain the same, unchanged by circumstance and time.

Emily Berry

To Bring You My Love by P J Harvey (1995)

I first saw P J Harvey performing in 1996 at the LA2 in central London, a venue that is now a ghost of polluted air hovering above a building site on Charing Cross Road. As I remember it she was wearing a bright-yellow jumpsuit and made that outfit live up to its name by springing about all over the stage like a cricket who had taken on the form of a divine woman. Sometime before that I'd bought a second-hand copy of *To Bring You My Love* on CD; it had a luxurious matt inlay sleeve depicting Harvey drowning like Ophelia in the Millais painting. Her songs were so furious and bereft they immediately reached inside me and coloured all my loneliest parts red. Caught between deserts and floods, her music seemed not only to understand life's emergency but to be powered by it.

I turned fifteen in 1996, and a teenager is in need of a war cry even if they don't know yet what their particular war will be. I had begun to suspect that heartbreak was in some ways a permanent condition, and if it was, how much better if that agony could be made gorgeous and baroque. For a long time I thought the lyric about cursing God in the title song was invoking the 'coastguard above', which seems fitting for an album that speaks to your most shipwrecked feelings; though if the god in *To Bring You My Love* is a coastguard, he's an unusually sadistic one, with little concern for whether his charges are waving or drowning. The American poet Mary Ruefle declared that a poem 'is supposed to be preparing me for my death'; I'd say the same is true of songs, and P J Harvey's are among the very best at it.

All those evenings spent listening to *To Bring You My Love* in my bedroom took me to the edge of something, and this must be how it gave me – as the kids say these days – so much life.

Erica Wagner

All Around My Hat by Steeleye Span (1975)

I would have been seven, going on eight. I feel as if I remember exactly where I was standing, that summer afternoon. In the warm sun porch of a house in Little Compton, Rhode Island, towards the eastern edge of the North American continent, the wild Atlantic just beyond. I was staying with my school friend Elizabeth. Her father Richard was, officially, the Coolest Dad in the Class. He wore turtleneck sweaters instead of ties; he was an artist who painted whales, sharks and squid. He had designed the great blue whale that hung in the American Museum of Natural History, haunt of our Manhattan childhoods. I feel as if I can see him laying the album on the turntable, lifting the needle, placing it on the disc. A cappella, a chorus of voices, a bold tune of lost love and courage, a song of longing and abandonment and hope.

Why should a song like that speak to a seven-year-old? I have no idea. But nothing – truly – was ever the same for me again.

Memory plays tricks. 'All Around My Hat' isn't the first track on Steeleye Span's eighth album, released in the autumn of 1975; that's 'Black Jack Davy'. Perhaps Richard dropped the needle onto the title song; perhaps that's what I choose to recall, four and a half decades later. I can't explain what happened to me that summer afternoon – only that, while still a little girl, I heard what I needed to hear, and my life turned to follow a sound.

Maddy Prior's soaring voice – as clear and clean in the twenty-first century, incidentally, as ever it was – took me into the spare, bold tales of the ballad tradition. They are tales of darkness, brilliance and magic; of abandoned lovers and cruel mothers; of enchantment, transformation and revenge. I saved my pocket money and bought the album for myself, gazing sideways at the anamorphic projections on its cover. I listened to it, the rhythms of folk with the drive of rock, the swing of fiddle, the energy of bass and drums, until the record's grooves flattened, or so it seemed. One thing led to another, as one thing usually does: before long I discovered the work of dozens of other artists, old and new, who continue to keep the folk tradition alive, and to remind us of the role the music of the people has played in protest and resistance through the ages. ('Hard Times of Old England', the second song on the album, stands up pretty well.)

I was a New York girl through and through, but ten years after I heard that record, I crossed the wild Atlantic myself and settled here in Britain, the source of the songs that made my life. I'll never leave. The music of this place runs through my blood.

Ali Smith

Various artists

Trying to choose one album about which to write this piece has made a week-long mutiny happen inside my head: now that I sit down to write it, *Court and Spark* and *Blue* by Joni Mitchell are already swinging boho punches at each other about which matters more; Kate and Anna McGarrigle's first album is giving me a sidelong witty French-Canadian look and surround-sounding the gorgeous unearthly harmony of the end of 'Heart Like a Wheel' at me so I'll know I couldn't ever choose to leave it on a sideline; then Elvis Costello's *My Aim Is True*, pointing right at me and shouting my name; Rickie Lee Jones's first album turning away shrugging like it always knew it was too cool for me anyway; and look at my young self waiting to see what her older self'll say about what Cat Stevens's *Tea for the Tillerman* and *Teaser and the Firecat* have come to mean in the shifts of time.

And, on my way home to write this, I pass a busker on the street playing 'I Am a Rock' and in come Simon & Garfunkel, all tragedy and adolescence, pure, raw *Sounds of Silence*. Then there's Nina Simone's *Black Gold* and my older brothers and sisters all coming up the stairs to hear what I was playing; and *Pillows & Prayers*, the Cherry Red compilation that meant I first heard Tracey Thorn and Ben Watt and ordered their solo albums at the Other Record Shop in a state of real excitement, and what about the excitement of hearing they'd teamed up? *Eden*, all cool horns and keys and undercurrents, a new kind of cosmopolitan, the sound of young adulthood, alongside Orange Juice's *You Can't Hide Your Love Forever*. This is the sound of happiness. And now, look up, Nick Drake's *Pink Moon* looming, melancholy, true. Which will you go for? Which will you love the best?

They're all playing at once. Turn the tables. That's my whole week gone, and the best part of four decades lost and found, going round and round.

CONTRIBUTORS

Emily Berry is the author of two poetry collections, *Dear Boy* and *Stranger, Baby*, which won the Forward Prize for best first collection in 2013. She edits *The Poetry Review*.

Billy Bragg is a singer-songwriter, activist and author whose books include *The Three Dimensions of Freedom* and *A Lover Sings: Selected Lyrics*.

John Burnside is a Scottish poet, novelist, memoirist and critic. His collection *Black Cat Bone* won both the T. S. Eliot Prize and the Forward Prize for best collection.

Jonathan Coe is a novelist whose books include *What a Carve Up!*, *The Rotters' Club* and *Middle England*. He also plays guitar and keyboards and released an album, *Unnecessary Music*, in 2015.

Teju Cole is a Nigerian–American novelist, essayist and photographer whose books include *Every Day Is for the Thief* and *Open City*.

Jason Cowley is the editor-in-chief of the *New Statesman* and the author of books including *The Last Game* and an essay collection, *Reaching for Utopia*.

Joe Dunthorne is a novelist and poet. His first book, *Submarine*, was made into a film in 2010.

Esi Edugyan is a Canadian author who has been shortlisted for the Booker Prize twice, most recently for her third novel, *Washington Black*.

Mark Ellen is a journalist and broadcaster who has edited magazines including *Smash Hits*, *Select*, *Mojo* and *The Word*. His memoir, *Rock Stars Stole My Life!*, was published in 2014.

Bernardine Evaristo is a novelist, poet and critic. Her eighth book, *Girl, Woman, Other*, was the joint winner of the 2019 Booker Prize.

Neil Gaiman is the author of novels, comics, children's books and screenplays including *The Sandman*, *Coraline* and *Good Omens*.

Linda Grant is a novelist and journalist. Her second book, *When I Lived in Modern Times*, won the Orange Prize in 2000.

Lavinia Greenlaw is a prize-winning poet and novelist and the author of a memoir, *The Importance of Music to Girls*.

Bonnie Greer is an American–British playwright, novelist, critic and broadcaster. Her books include the memoirs *Obama Music* and *A Parallel Life*.

Sarah Hall is a prize-winning novelist and short-story writer whose books include *The Carhullan Army* and *Sudden Traveller*. In 2013, she was named one of Granta's twenty best young British novelists.

John Harris is a journalist and critic whose books include *The Last Party: Britpop, Blair and the Demise of English Rock*.

Will Harris is a writer of mixed Anglo-Indonesian heritage. He is the author of a book-length essay, *Mixed-Race Superman*, and a poetry collection, *RENDANG*, which won the Forward Prize for best first collection in 2020.

Melissa Harrison is a novelist and nature writer whose third novel, *All Among the Barley*, was the UK winner of the EU Prize for Literature in 2019.

David Hepworth is a journalist, broadcaster, magazine publisher and author whose bestselling books include *A Fabulous Creation: How the LP Saved Our Lives*.

Clive James was a broadcaster, poet, critic, memoirist and songwriter. He published several acclaimed poetry collections during a long illness before he died in 2019.

Marlon James was born in Jamaica and lives in the United States. He is the author of five novels, including *A Brief History of Seven Killings*, which won the Booker Prize in 2015.

Alan Johnson was Labour MP for Kingston upon Hull West and Hessle from 1997 to 2017; he served as education secretary, health secretary and home secretary. He is the prize-winning author of four books including *In My Life: A Music Memoir*.

Daisy Johnson is a novelist and short-story writer. She became the youngest writer ever to be shortlisted for the Booker Prize with *Everything Under* in 2018.

Rachel Kushner is an American author whose books include *The Mars Room*, shortlisted for the Booker Prize in 2018, and an essay collection, *The Hard Crowd*.

Olivia Laing is a prize-winning writer and critic. She is the author of four non-fiction books, a novel and an essay collection, *Funny Weather*.

Deborah Levy is a novelist and playwright. Her books include the memoir *The Cost of Living* and the Booker-shortlisted novels *Swimming Home* and *Hot Milk*.

Patricia Lockwood is an American author and critic. She is the author of a poetry collection, *Motherland Fatherland Homelandsexuals*, a memoir, *Priestdaddy*, and a novel, *No One Is Talking About This*.

Sabrina Mahfouz was raised in London and Cairo. She is an award-winning poet, playwright and librettist whose plays include *With a Little Bit of Luck*, a celebration of UK garage music.

Eimear McBride was born in Ireland and lives in London. Her debut novel, *A Girl Is a Half-formed Thing*, won the Goldsmiths Prize and the Baileys Women's Prize for fiction.

David Mitchell is the Booker-shortlisted author of nine novels, including *Cloud Atlas*, which was made into a film in 2012. He wrote dialogue for Kate Bush's 2014 live show, *Before the Dawn*.

Suzanne Moore is a journalist and columnist who has written for publications including *Marxism Today*, the *Mail on Sunday*, the *Guardian* and the *New Statesman*. In 2019 she was joint winner of the Orwell Prize for journalism.

Kate Mossman is a journalist and broadcaster whose BBC documentaries include *When Pop Ruled My Life: The Fans' Story*. She is a senior writer at the *New Statesman*.

Fiona Mozley is the author of two novels: her debut, *Elmet*, which was shortlisted for the Booker Prize in 2017, and *Hot Stew*.

Neel Mukherjee was born in India and lives in London. He is the author of three novels; his second, *The Lives of Others*, was shortlisted for the Booker Prize in 2014.

Daljit Nagra is a prize-winning poet. His books include the collections *Look We Have Coming to Dover!* and *British Museum*, and a retelling of the *Ramayana*.

Ben Okri was born in Nigeria and lives in London. He has published poems, short stories, essays and eleven novels, including *The Famished Road*, which won the Booker Prize in 1991.

Musa Okwonga is a poet, journalist, musician and football writer based in Berlin. His most recent book is *One of Them: An Eton College Memoir*.

Sandeep Parmar was born in Nottingham and raised in Southern California. She is a critic, academic and award-winning poet whose books include *Eidolon* and *The Marble Orchard*.

Sarah Perry is the prize-winning author of three novels: *After Me Comes the Flood*, *The Essex Serpent* and *Melmoth*.

Ian Rankin is a Scottish crime writer whose Inspector Rebus novels are international bestsellers. He is the singer in the band Best Picture.

Meg Rosoff is an American writer based in London. She is the author of several young-adult novels including *How I Live Now* and *Just in Case*, which won the Carnegie Medal in 2007.

George Saunders is an American writer and academic. He is the author of four short-story collections and a novel, *Lincoln in the Bardo*, which won the Booker Prize in 2017.

Will Self is a journalist, broadcaster and novelist. He is the author of many books including a trilogy of modernist novels – *Umbrella*, *Shark* and *Phone* – and a memoir, *Will*.

Lionel Shriver is an American author and journalist who lives in London. Her novel *We Need to Talk About Kevin* won the Orange Prize and was made into a film in 2011.

Ali Smith was born in Inverness and lives in Cambridge. She is the award-winning author of five short-story collections and ten novels, including *How to Be Both* and the seasonal quartet that concluded with *Summer* in 2020.

Preti Taneja is a writer, academic and broadcaster. Her debut novel, *We That Are Young*, won the 2018 Desmond Elliott Prize.

Neil Tennant worked as a journalist for *Smash Hits* in the early 1980s while he made his first recordings with Chris Lowe as the Pet Shop Boys. A selection of his lyrics was published in 2018.

Tracey Thorn is a singer-songwriter, author and one half of the band Everything But The Girl. She has published four books, including the memoir *Bedsit Disco Queen*, and writes a fortnightly column in the *New Statesman*.

Colm Tóibín is an award-winning Irish writer whose novels include *The Master* and *Brooklyn*, which was made into a film in 2015.

Erica Wagner was born in New York and lives in London. Her books include *Chief Engineer: The Man Who Built the Brooklyn Bridge*. She is a contributing writer to the *New Statesman* and former literary editor of *The Times*.

COPYRIGHT INFORMATION

A Love Supreme by John Coltrane © John Harris, 2017 and 2021

This Year's Model by Elvis Costello © Meg Rosoff, 2017

Rachmaninov's *Piano Concertos Nos 2 and 4* performed by Sequeira Costa © Sarah Perry, 2017

The Man-Machine by Kraftwerk © Neil Tennant, 2021

Movements by Booka Shade © Melissa Harrison, 2021

Give a Damn by the Johnstons © Colm Tóibín, 2021

Selections 1976–1988 by Sweet Honey in the Rock © Bernardine Evaristo, 2017

A Symphony of Amaranths by Neil Ardley © Jonathan Coe, 2017

Revolver by the Beatles © Alan Johnson, 2017

Regulate . . . G Funk Era by Warren G © Will Harris, 2021

Cheap Thrills by Big Brother and the Holding Company © Bonnie Greer, 2017

Blue by Joni Mitchell © David Mitchell, 2017 and 2021

OK Computer by Radiohead © Sarah Hall, 2021

Cassadaga by Bright Eyes © Fiona Mozley, 2021

Maxinquaye by Tricky © Esi Edugyan, 2021

Sail Away by Randy Newman © David Hepworth, 2017 and 2021

Black Sunday by Cypress Hill © Joe Dunthorne, 2017

Fresh by Sly and the Family Stone © Suzanne Moore, 2017 and 2021

Kind of Blue by Miles Davis © Ben Okri, 2021

Automatic for the People by R.E.M. © Olivia Laing, 2021

Mozart's *Piano Concertos in D minor and A major* performed by Clara Haskil © Neel Mukherjee, 2021
Diamond Dogs by David Bowie © Neil Gaiman, 2021
Innervisions by Stevie Wonder © Tracey Thorn, 2017
Aquemini by Outkast © Musa Okwonga, 2017
The B-52's by the B-52's © Mark Ellen, 2017 and 2021
Hejira by Joni Mitchell © Linda Grant, 2017 and 2021
The Colour of Spring by Talk Talk © Jason Cowley, 2021
Astral Weeks by Van Morrison © Will Self, 2017 and 2021
A Little Deeper by Ms. Dynamite © Sabrina Mahfouz, 2021
A Natural Disaster by Anathema © John Burnside, 2017
Last Exit to Brooklyn by Mark Knopfler © Lionel Shriver, 2017
Meat Is Murder by the Smiths © Daljit Nagra, 2021
Mother Juno by the Gun Club © Rachel Kushner, 2021
Solid Air by John Martyn © Ian Rankin, 2017 and 2021
To Bring You My Love by P J Harvey © Emily Berry, 2017 and 2021
All Around My Hat by Steeleye Span © Erica Wagner, 2021
Various artists © Ali Smith, 2017 and 2021

NOTES

INTRODUCTION

1 *Michael Jackson: The Magic, the Madness, the Whole Story* by J. Randy Taraborrelli (Grand Central Publishing), p. 226.

2 *A Fabulous Creation: How the LP Saved Our Lives* by David Hepworth (Bantam Press), p. xviii.

3 https://www.loc.gov/collections/emile-berliner/articles-and-essays/emile-berliner-biography/

4 https://www.loc.gov/collections/emile-berliner/articles-and-essays/gramophone/

5 *The History of Music Production* by Richard James Burgess (OUP), p. 19.

6 *The Long-Player Goodbye: The Album from Vinyl to iPod and Back Again* by Travis Elborough (Sceptre), pp. 19–30. Nathan Milstein's performance of Mendelssohn's Violin Concerto in E Minor led Columbia's catalogue of 12-inch LPs.

7 *Tearing Down the Wall of Sound: The Rise and Fall of Phil Spector* by Mick Brown (A&C Black), p. 185.

8 John Cale, quoted in *Mojo* magazine, 'Beatles 101 Greatest Songs: Norwegian Wood', July 2006.

9 *Pet Sounds* by Jim Fusilli (Bloomsbury Continuum), pp. 79–80.

10 *Wouldn't It Be Nice: Brian Wilson and the Making of the Beach Boys' Pet Sounds* by Charles L. Granata, Tony Asher (Chicago Review Press).

11 *Revolution in the Head: The Beatles' Records and the Sixties* by Ian MacDonald (Pimlico), p. 215.

12 McCartney quoted in MacDonald, p. 232.

13 MacDonald, p. 249.

14 *Yeah Yeah Yeah: The Story of Modern Pop* by Bob Stanley (Faber & Faber), pp. 286–7.

15 https://www.juxtapoz.com/news/music/sound-and-vision-stanley-donwood-on-the-making-of-radiohead-s-the-bends-cover-art/

16 Hepworth, p. 252.

17 https://www.ft.com/content/f7b0f2b0-8009-11e2-adbd-00144feabdc0

18 https://www.riaa.com/u-s-sales-database/

19 https://www.ons.gov.uk/economy/inflationandpriceindices/timeseries/czms/mm23

20 Quoted in MacDonald, pp. 248–9.

21 MacDonald, p. 221.

22 *How Music Got Free: The End of an Industry, the Turn of the Century, and the Patient Zero of Piracy* by Stephen Witt (Viking), p. 6.

23 https://www.riaa.com/u-s-sales-database/

24 https://www.spin.com/2015/04/portishead-geoff-barrow-streaming-estimate-twitter/

25 https://www.theguardian.com/technology/2013/oct/07/spotify-thom-yorke-dying-corpse

26 https://musicbiz.org/wp-content/uploads/2018/09/AM_US_2018_V5.pdf

27 https://www.theguardian.com/music/2017/aug/17/they-could-destroy-the-album-how-spotify-playlists-have-changed-music-for-ever

28 https://www.bpi.co.uk/news-analysis/streaming-breaks-the-100-billion-barrier-fuelled-by-exciting-new-talent/

29 https://praguebusinessjournal.com/gz-media-turnover-up-5-over-czk-2-5-billion-in-2017/

ACKNOWLEDGEMENTS

This book would not have been possible without Jason Cowley and Kate Mossman, my colleagues at the *New Statesman*; I am grateful for their generosity and good judgement.

Thanks to those who brought this book to life with such enthusiasm: my agent, Antony Harwood; Michael Fishwick, Lilidh Kendrick, Sarah Ruddick, David Mann, Emma Bal and Anna Massardi at Bloomsbury; and Martin O'Neill, whose inspired cover art began as an equally inspired commission by my *NS* colleague Gerry Brakus.

Thanks to all the writers who gave generously of their time and craft and readily shared their personal histories. Thanks, too, to the agents and assistants who helped smooth the way: Tracy Bohan, Charlie Coletta, Rebecca Eskildsen, Anna Haddelsey, Jenny Hewson, David Hutchins, Robert Kirby, Becky Thomas, Martha Wydysh, Kathy Rong Zhou and Alba Ziegler-Bailey.

Thanks to David Hepworth, Dan Papps and Jon Savage for sound advice, to Philip Oltermann for invaluable edits and to Erica Wagner for a constant supply of wisdom. Thanks to Martin Colthorpe at International Literature

Festival Dublin for letting me spin Joni Mitchell and David Bowie records with David Mitchell and Deborah Levy in 2018.

Thanks to my parents, Annie and Will, for bringing me up in a house filled with good books and even better records; my sister, Georgia, for the car-journey singalongs; my friend Mark for sharing his headphones at the back of 4F; and my children, Verette and John, for occasionally letting me choose the tunes.

And thank you Claire, the best dancer, record-shop-browser and mix-maker as well as the finest reader, editor and listener I could hope for. Here's to Side Two.

A NOTE ON THE AUTHOR

Tom Gatti is deputy editor of the *New Statesman*, where *Long Players* began life as a feature. He joined the magazine in 2013 as culture editor; before that he was Saturday Review editor at *The Times*, where he also wrote book reviews, features and interviews. From 1995 to the present, he has listened to Radiohead's *The Bends* more times than is strictly necessary.

A NOTE ON THE TYPE

The text of this book is set in Minion, a digital typeface designed by Robert Slimbach in 1990 for Adobe Systems. The name comes from the traditional naming system for type sizes, in which minion is between nonpareil and brevier. It is inspired by late Renaissance-era type.